ALL AROUND THE WORLD THIS SIMPLE TEACHING IS TRANSFORMING LIVES . . .

Australia

On the shelves of Christian bookstores today I see a growing number of books exploring the subject of the Father heart of God. This is a good thing, as it seems to me it is a truth which the church has somewhat neglected, yet so desperately needs to hear and receive. Ken Symington has been teaching about God as Father for many years, and I have experienced firsthand – both in my own life and observing the lives of the people who come to the "Father Heart of God" weekend courses which Ken runs – radical transformation at the core of a person's being. Through Ken's clear Biblical insight, and his own powerful testimony, we get to know the Dad we always yearned for, and to be opened to all the possibilities that can be ours when we catch the truth that we are His precious sons and daughters.

Rev. Paul Watson, Regional Director, Ellel Ministries Australia

England

The understanding that Almighty God is our Daddy – which Ken Symington so vividly portrays in this book – powerfully impacts the lives of so many in this fatherless generation. There has never been a time when this truth was more urgently needed than it is now. I have seen this teaching totally transform many lives and this book can do the same for you!

Jill Southern, Director, Ellel Pierrepont, England

Germany

We have been mightily blessed through Ken's "Father Heart of God" teaching into a fatherless society. German society is still struggling from the consequences of the last war when the nation was infiltrated by false fatherhood, when many people lost fathers, and when those fathers who did survive came back with very damaged and suppressed emotions. Even after three generations this message is still very vital. Many men are still closed up emotionally and need much releasing. They need to hear God's truth on fatherhood. For many the message is a real eye-opener and a step into a new depth of relationship with God as their Father, and into a new dimension of being fathers themselves. The truth about real fatherhood and sonship has the potential to move mountains, and many have responded very readily to the invitations and the challenges. There is a determination when the hunger for the real thing is awakened. A very timely and vital message for the German people.

Andreas Hefti, Director, Ellel Germany

Hungary

I'm certain that this book will touch many hearts. For me personally, it was life-transforming. In this fatherless age there is a desperate cry for God the Father's love. A father's love and tender care is something we were supposed to get, but too often we did not receive it.

Tamas Kovacs, Director, Ellel Ministries Hungary

Ireland (Northern)

One of the most powerful truths that every child of God needs to experience – and not just intellectually – is that God is love.

We learn to love because God is love, and we cannot love out to others until we have received His love into ourselves. The power of this truth is foundational to everything we think and believe as children of God.

As a pastor of a twenty-first-century church, I have experienced how

Ken Symington's teaching on the Father heart of God has caused many rejected and hurting people to flourish and blossom as they discover for themselves that their deepest need and the cry of their hearts is met and fulfilled in Abba Father, our awesome Daddy God. I wholeheartedly recommend this book as a foundational truth, leading to completeness in Christ.

Jeff Wright, Senior Pastor, Green Pastures,
Ballymena, Northern Ireland

Ireland (Southern)

I have been working with the drug- and alcohol-addicted for many years. When I had a life-changing encounter on Ken's "Father Heart of God" weekend, I knew that I had to use this as a way of reaching the broken and the addicted. Drug addicts and alcoholics, 99% of the time, have had no real fathering, so when they discover that God is and wants to be their Dad it does something to their hearts. They slowly learn to love and trust again. Ken Symington has become like a spiritual father to us here and I know this book will be powerful, as he is anointed to impart this truth to others.

Philip Richardson, Lifeline Recovery, Ireland

Sweden

I have had the privilege of translating a few times for Ken Symington when he has given his course "The Father Heart of God" in Sweden. Standing with the speaker on the podium gives you a vantage point to observe the reactions of those attending. It has always been a joy to see how people have received what Ken has given them. To many it has very obviously been a revelation of something they have never heard of before; others have begun to grasp more fully what to them has seemed too good to be true – that their Heavenly Father is altogether good, in all He does, and not just a copy of the imperfect fathers most of us have grown up with. As Ken has been teaching, with humor and easy-to-understand examples, I have seen faces change from disbelief to surprise to hope. And when at the end of the course the call has been given to seek a place at the front of the hall, and just sit there to be with the Father, there has always been a quiet walk up front, and in quietness many of God's children have discovered what they never had known: They have a Father who is worth knowing for what He really is. They have sat there, sometimes for hours, just enjoying Him, just like children on their father's lap. For many, that has been the beginning of an entirely new understanding of, and a new walk with, their Father God.

As this teaching now comes in the form of a book, may it reach many more, to bring hope, healing, and restoration to those who have suffered from a distorted picture of what a father is, and have never been able to know and enjoy the blessing of a full relationship with their Heavenly Father!

Goran Andersson, Director, Ellel Sweden

LOVED LIKE
NEVER BEFORE

LOVED LIKE NEVER BEFORE

*Discovering the Father
Heart of God*

Ken Symington

Sovereign World

Sovereign World Ltd
PO Box 784
Ellel
Lancaster LA1 9DA
England

www.sovereignworld.com

ISBN 978 1 85240 585 4

Book cover design by The Book Design Company
Typeset by The Book Design Company
Printed in the United Kingdom

CONTENTS

Thank you, Linda, for being with me
every step of the way

FOREWORD

A part from the truth that we are saved by grace through faith in Jesus Christ, there is no greater message than that of knowing how much Father God loves you.

Here at Ellel Ministries near Sydney, Australia, we run many weekend seminars and conferences every year, and one of the first events to go into our calendar each year is the "Father Heart of God" course. It is a crucial teaching. We have flown Ken Symington out from Northern Ireland almost every year to impart this vital subject since our inception. Why? Because unless we can help disciples understand the Father's heart for themselves, all we will do is raise *slaves*, rather than *sons*. Romans 8:19 states:

> The creation waits in eager expectation for the sons of God to be revealed.

The raising of true "sons" is impossible, unless we can introduce them properly to their Heavenly Father.

And why Ken Symington? If I could find someone else on the planet who could communicate this essential message better than Ken,

I would fly-in that person to speak instead, but I have not yet found anyone who can teach it or model it better.

To now have this teaching in print is an answer to prayer. Ken has a brilliant ability to respond to the often-posed query: "I know God loves me in my head, but how do I get it into my heart?" This book will answer that question for many people.

More than anybody else I know, Ken Symington has a gift for drawing those who are timid, fearful, abused, rejected, and abandoned, to a place where they can receive the Father's love for the very first time. This truth transforms their faith in God by revealing Him as a gentle, loving, kind, and safe Father. It also forever changes a person's ability to serve in the Kingdom, now as a son or daughter of God, rather than as a "performance-oriented slave." No believer can find their true identity or destiny until this message has become planted deep within them.

However good you thought Abba Father was, this book will prove He's even better than you first suspected!

Paul Ryan
Center Director
"Gilbulla"
Ellel Ministries
Sydney, Australia

Introduction

I have been in full-time Christian ministry as a teacher for nearly fifteen years, traveling to many parts of the world and teaching on a wide variety of subjects. I have often said that if God asked me to teach on only one subject for the rest of my life and gave me the choice, I would choose "The Father Heart of God." That is because I have seen this simple teaching change more lives than all the other teachings in total.

Here it is in three words: "God loves you."

Ah, but you already know that, don't you? If you were stopped in the high street this weekend by someone with a clipboard who asked the question, "Does God love you?" you would confidently answer, "Yes." But in my experience this usually represents head-knowledge rather than heart-knowledge.

Here's a test. Imagine the following for a moment.

The angel Gabriel appears to you and says that God would like to see you in His office. Behind Gabriel you see three impressive doors. One marked "God the Father," one marked "Jesus Christ," and one marked "Holy Spirit."

"Which door shall I go to?" you ask Gabriel.

"Any one," he replies.

You stand and look at the three doors set in front of you. Your head-knowledge tells you that it shouldn't matter which door. God is One and yet Three (in the mystery of the Trinity). There should be no difference. After all, Jesus said that He and the Father are one, and that he who has seen Him has seen the Father, with the Apostle Paul affirming this profound truth again and again.[1]

And yet.

And yet you would gladly knock on the middle door where Jesus would be. Maybe at a push you might knock on the third door marked "Holy Spirit," not entirely sure what might happen in there. But the last door, definitely the last door that you would delightedly knock on would be that of "God the Father."

Because you know what fathers are like, don't you?

If that would be your reaction, then please read this book. It is my prayer, and the very heart of God, that by the end of the book your new response would be a desire to run to the first door with childlike delight, knowing that you will be truly welcomed, loved, and valued.

That you belong there.

That you are safe there.

Ken Symington

Notes

1. John 10:30; 14:9–10; Colossians 1:15; Hebrews 1:3.

CHAPTER 1

THE WORD "FATHER" IS NOT NEUTRAL

Some years ago I received a phone call from an elderly couple who had one of my teaching tapes in their possession (in the good old days before CDs). They had joined in with the prayer at the end of the teaching, and as the wife was praying, she began to receive a measure of healing. However, the tape suddenly ended halfway through the prayer, and the lady concluded that if she could just hear the other half, she might receive complete healing.

On hearing their dilemma, I readily agreed to go round to their home and finish the prayer with them.

The husband and wife who greeted me were longstanding Christians. The reason I mention this is to make the point that these were not young, inexperienced Christians; they were deeply committed and long-serving members of the Body of Christ. At the end of the evening, after we had dealt with the issue at hand, we sat down for some tea and biscuits. They invited me to "give thanks" to God, and I happily obliged. However, when I looked up after praying, I noticed they both had tears in their eyes.

I asked them why they had been touched so deeply in their emotions by my short prayer of thanksgiving, and they answered, "Because we don't know the Father."

I then realized that when I had given thanks, I must have started by saying, "Dear Daddy God . . ." (I don't always start my prayers with "Dear Daddy God." Sometimes I say, "Dear Sovereign God Almighty," or use a similar formal title, but this time I must have started with "Dear Daddy God.") The intimacy with which I knew God the Father had obviously struck that emotional chord.

Had they been new believers who were only a few weeks into their walk with God, this would not have been a surprise. But for two godly "saints" who had been used powerfully by God for decades in the healing ministry to say, "We don't know God the Father" – that was a shock to me.

Instinctively I said to them, "Tell me about your own fathers." Strangely, their stories were almost identical. Their fathers had both been very busy men. They were distant figures who went out to work in the morning and came back at night, only to go straight into a side room to read a newspaper. They would later appear for dinner, but would say very little, clearly indicating to all that their minds were firmly fixed on other things. Finally, they would disappear again, going off to do some other work on their own for the rest of the evening. Both fathers had been like ships passing in the night.

I asked if their fathers had ever taken an interest in their schoolwork or indeed in anything else that was a part of their young lives. "No," they informed me; their fathers were always too busy to take any interest in what they did inside or outside of school. I then asked if their fathers had ever shown them any affection. Again, their answer was "No." Their fathers never showed them any affection.

Suddenly, for the first time, I realized that the word "father" is not a neutral word.

To illustrate this point, let me tell you a story – something that happened to me many years ago.

As a young man, I and a friend called Peter would travel to the coast of Northern Ireland during the summer months to catch mackerel. These fish arrive around the shores of the British Isles every year in their millions, making them very easy fish to catch.

During one such Saturday outing, we were at a small fishing village in County Down called Ardglass. Having managed to rent a rowing boat for the day, we rowed half a mile along the coast to a point underneath some cliffs. The sun was shining, the water was flat calm, and it wasn't long before Peter and I started catching fish after fish. Soon the boat was well laden down with dozens of freshly caught mackerel.

The idyllic setting was interrupted by two small shark fins that surfaced about 400 meters from the boat. As Ireland (perhaps understandably) does not have many sharks, we decided to put the fishing on hold for a while and try to get a better look at these two small specimens. We slowly manhandled our rented 17-foot rowing boat towards the two fins but, in doing so, managed to break one of the two oars. The weather being as peaceful as it was, this didn't present any real danger – as one oar would be enough to get us back to the harbor. However, as we now had only one oar between us, we gave up the shark chase and carried on removing mackerel from the Irish Sea.

Suddenly – and if there was a stronger word than "suddenly" I would use it – a huge dorsal fin rose up alongside the boat. As I stared in disbelief, I saw the huge fin slowly topple over, then slowly straighten up again. Neither Peter nor I were shark experts but we did know that only a huge shark could have such a huge fin! And as if things could not get worse, another large fin rose out of the water, this time at the back of the boat. When I carefully peered over the side, it became clear that it had not been two small sharks we had seen earlier – it had been one massive beast. It was as long as our 17-foot boat and easily measured a meter across its back.

I was not a Christian at the time, but with reflection I am sure that if someone had appeared at that very moment and asked me to say the Sinner's Prayer, I would have done so with all my heart. We were in trouble.

The monster shark stationed itself alongside our boat with its gigantic mouth in the wide-open position, just waiting. Was I going to be the next Jonah?

As panic quickly set in, Peter and I held emergency whispered discussions on what to do next. I came to the conclusion that the shark must have smelt the many fish in the boat, so I suggested that we throw the fish overboard one at a time, and while the shark was busy chasing and consuming our catch we could make our getaway, albeit slowly, back to safety. Peter, in his wisdom, threw doubt on my plan by asking what would happen when we ran out of mackerel and the monster realized that our little boat was the rich source of this easy food. (Good point. Hadn't thought of that!)

I told Peter I had read somewhere that if you hit a shark on the nose it will definitely swim away. He wasn't convinced. Deep down, neither was I.

Then I had an awful thought. A horrible thought. But under the circumstances, it seemed a clever thought. It went like this: If I leaned rather quickly to the side of the boat to look at the shark again, the boat would rock to that side, and Peter might sort of, *unbalance*, and . . . Well, I think you get the idea! (Don't get religious on me – you weren't there!)

However, I caught a strange look in Peter's eye and I realized that fearful minds think alike, so another plan faded.

After what seemed like an eternity, the shark, of its own accord, sank slowly back down into the depths from which it had come. Seizing our opportunity, Peter took the one remaining good oar, lodged himself at the front end of the boat, and started to pull us slowly, one side at a time, on the seemingly endless half-mile journey back to the safety of the harbor. Meanwhile, I took the other oar, broken as it was, and, kneeling on the back seat, held it high above my head, ready to strike if the beast should return. I would not go down without a fight.

The fact that you are reading my account of the event shows that we safely reached the harbor from whence we had come a few hours earlier. (You need to take my word for it that Peter made it back!)

Once back on dry land, and out for a few pints with our friends that evening, the story of the encounter with the giant shark proved very popular. We were heroes among our peers – and of course as young men in our early twenties it felt good. The shark was huge, but it may have grown somewhat as we recounted the tale of our bravery, leaving out the cowardly discussion and thoughts outlined above.

We were heroes indeed, until the Monday morning regional newspaper was published. A front-page sub-headline, at first glance, confirmed our story: "GIANT 17-FOOT SHARK WASHED UP AT ARDGLASS." Further reading, however, informed the readers that it was not the man-eating monster we had presumed it to be, and had described it as, but a toothless, gentle, inquisitive, completely harmless basking shark which lived solely on plankton.

Our hero status was over. And we were the butt of many jokes for quite a while. (Had any nasty sucks from any sharks recently?)

The fact is that most words are neutral. Words such as "carpet," "chair," or "tree" will not raise any heartbeat. If I walked along a crowded Australian beach in summer and shouted, "Sand! Sand!" then I wouldn't expect to see a response from anyone. However, if I then shouted, "Shark! Shark!" a mass stampede would probably occur.

Words such as "shark," "murder," "rape," and "cancer" definitely carry with them an unspoken power. These words are not neutral, because we associate them with power to harm us. In my experience, the most powerful non-neutral word is the word "father."

If you are alive, you had a father. That doesn't mean you had a dad, but you did have a father. Your own life experience of a "father," whether good or bad, greatly colors that word to the extent that "father" is no longer just another word. It contains delight or dread, security or fear, acceptance or rejection.

God could have called Himself anything He wanted. No title would be too exaggerated to describe the Creator of the universe. Yet Jesus referred to Him as "our Father,"[1] or more often as "your Father."[2]

Whether we realize it or not, when it comes to relating to the word "father" we have invisible glasses on. To some, a father is someone to keep at a distance; to others, a father is someone to run to when you feel threatened. It is with these same glasses that most people look to God "the Father."

A lady that I know wrote the following poem. She has struggled desperately in her bid to know God, trust God, and not to be terrified by the prospect of meeting Him. Her father's behavior, as you will read, has had a profound effect on how she sees herself and how she sees "Father God." She gave her life to Jesus at a church meeting when she was a little girl aged around ten or eleven, but, as you will read in the fourth verse, when she told her father what she had done, he tried to beat it out of her.

> *Daddy, what went wrong? I was supposed to be the apple*
> *of your eye!*
> *Yet all I have are memories of how you made me cry.*
> *You never told me what I did wrong to make you hate*
> *me so,*
> *I couldn't change the things I did, because I didn't know!*
>
> *I tried so hard to please you, so you'd love me, just a bit,*
> *But we were like a hand inside a glove that didn't fit.*
> *Why did you take me out my bed, and put me in the shed?*
> *So many times the things you did left me wishing I*
> *was dead.*
>
> *Most days you said you wished you had a dog instead*
> *of me,*
> *I tried to hide the tears I cried, so you couldn't see.*
> *You did so many crazy things, going wild with your*
> *loaded gun,*
> *It frightened me, the things you did, and you stole all*
> *my fun.*

When I said I'd gave my life to God, it made you hate
me more,
You used to grab me by my hair and pull me to the floor.
You'd kick me many times to make me say God was not real,
But at that time, nothing you did could take away the joy
I'd feel.

Then I heard God was a Father, and that just filled my life
with fears,
It made me want to run and hide, so much screaming,
shouting, tears.
How can God be my Daddy, and love me, if you couldn't!
I tried so hard to please you and not do the things I shouldn't.

No lights, no heating, some days no food, and no pictures
on our wall,
We lived in total fear of the time when from the pub
you'd crawl.
We felt like prisoners in your house, a place so cold and cruel,
We weren't allowed to get it right because you kept changing
all the rules.

But they tell me God's not like you – He loves me,
He really does!
And all the things you did to me, they broke His heart
because
To Him my life is precious; He doesn't want to punish me,
He wants to take away my pain, so at last I can be free.
He wants to give me back my smile, He wants to show me
how to live.
He wants to wrap me in His arms, He has so much He
wants to give.

*Only, Dad, the things you did to me, they hurt me deep
inside,
And trusting God to love me is so hard, I know. I've tried!
Why could you never love me? You never sat me on your knee,
I missed you so much, Daddy, but you just wait and see!*

*One day God will help me; He will take me by the hand,
He'll take me from the darkness, into a whole new land.
A land where I will find my peace! And know His love
inside,
Where at last I will feel safe and no longer want to hide.
A place where I can lift my head and no longer feel
the shame,
A place where I'll have a right to live with joy instead
of pain.*

*I don't know when God will touch my life, but I'm sure He's
made a start,
He sent some friends to teach me now about His Father's
heart.
So Daddy, I don't need you, one day God will be my Dad,
And I will know a Daddy's love, a love I've never had.*

*The way is really scary; I so want to believe it's true,
But I guess nothing can be as scary as the "love" I got
from you!
When I know that God is with me, and I have no more tears
to cry,
Then I will somehow find your grave, and I will come to
say "Goodbye."
Though you've been dead now many years, you are still a
part of me,
But not for long, your time is up, and soon I will be free!*

Free from all the hurting and the pain that stole my life,
Free to grow into a "grown-up," a mother, and a wife.
No longer feeling like a child, the screaming will be gone,
The fear of you broken, so at last I can move on.

I don't know how God can take this mess, but I've been told
He can,
Because all the things you did to me, they weren't part of
His plan.
The plans He has are good for me, though I don't know
the way,
He will take me by the hand, and show me every day.

On wings just like an eagle, I will soar with Him on high,
Like a bird set free from its cage, at last I'll learn to fly.
And He will be my Daddy, a Daddy who loves me so,
He'll stay by my side forever, and teach me the way to go.
He will fill my life with good things, things I've never known!
Then one day when I meet Him, He'll say, "My child, you're
safely home!"

(Dee Smith, 2004 – used with permission)

It is tough reading, but it helps to firmly establish the essential starting point for this journey of discovery, that the word "father" is not a neutral word.

WHAT DOES THE WORD "FATHER" MEAN TO YOU?

Here is a selection of words that it might be helpful to reflect on, and perhaps circle accordingly if they ring true in your experience.

⁘ Security	⁘ Stranger
⁘ Fear	⁘ Friend
⁘ Safe	⁘ Listener
⁘ Violent	⁘ For you
⁘ Fun	⁘ Distant
⁘ Protection	⁘ Loving
⁘ Help	⁘ Bully

What conclusion have you reached? Do you see Father God with the same words attached to Him?

Notes

1. Matthew 6:9.
2. Matthew 5:16, 45, 48; 6:4.

CHAPTER 2

MY OWN "FATHER" STORY

I was blessed, truly blessed, to have a brilliant mum and dad. Our family was, and still is, an incredibly close-knit family, right out to nephews and nieces. But this is about fathers, and to understand my story you need to understand my father.

My father was very intelligent, and loved learning, but as a boy from a poor family he never had the opportunity of a good education. At the age of fourteen he had to leave school and find work in order to help the family finances. He worked for a shoe wholesaler by day, and in the evening he put rugs over the handlebars of his bicycle and sold them from door to door.

He married my mum in 1945 and I was born during one of the coldest winters on record, in December 1947. Two sisters followed in due course, each three years apart.

By this time my father had opened a small shoe shop in the working-class area of East Belfast. It was a horrible, cold, and sometimes damp building on the Albertbridge Road, squeezed between a pawnbroker and a baker. He sold cheap shoes to a community that was always financially challenged. He loved the people but hated every day in that shop.

As he grew older he developed a love for antiques, philosophy, theology, and natural history. He bought books by the hundreds, and at his death we had an estimated 4,000 volumes in the attic of our home. My dad was a Christian from an early age, and though there were times when he questioned aspects of his faith, he always held fast to it. He said that the fulfilled prophecies, especially the rebirth of Israel in 1948, confirmed his faith in God's Word. He knew his Bible inside out and often stood in for church ministers when they were on holiday.

The shoe shop just about provided enough income for the family to live in a rented house, own one very old second-hand car, and go once every few years for a week-long holiday in the South of Ireland. My parents never owned a house or a new car.

So it is no surprise that my dad had big aspirations for his firstborn son. His son would have the educational opportunities that he had been denied. His son would have the opportunity to go to university, perhaps becoming a doctor or a lawyer.

Problem was, his firstborn son had almost zero interest in school.

At age eleven, I somehow passed the first filter examination called the "11-plus." This entitled me to have a "grammar school" education – which was designed to lead pupils to university – rather than a "secondary school" education, which was designed to lead to a trade. My father was extremely proud of my exam pass and wanted me to choose one of three top grammar schools in Belfast. But I knew that academia was not my gifting and, to his disappointment, I pretty much insisted that I attend a nearby grammar school that was not well regarded academically (and in fact no longer exists).

The next filter examination was called the "Junior" exam. It appeared on your horizon when you reached the age of fourteen and was designed to check that you were on track for university-level education. Three years later you would then sit the "Senior" exam, which was your entry exam for university itself.

The Junior by today's standard was a strange exam. You sat all the usual subjects such as physics, chemistry, biology, geography, history, art, French, English (comprehension and written), and mathematics (including trigonometry). However, even if you got a pass in most of these subjects, if you failed in either English or mathematics you failed the Junior. It was largely unspoken, but in truth you understood that failure deemed you as unlikely to be university material.

I knew I would fail Junior because I went fishing on the day of the mathematics tests. Trigonometry in particular was like a foreign language to me.

I knew my father would be annoyed when, in due time, he would be told that I had failed, but I reckoned I could handle that. He could be a bit fiery at times, so I imagined that he would be angry for a few hours, and then normal life would continue.

How wrong I was, and how unprepared for his reaction!

He opened the envelope on exam results day and stared at the small page it contained. In the appropriate results box someone had written a large "F" in black fountain-pen ink (I found the page a few years ago). I braced myself for a short fiery outburst, but it didn't come. He set the envelope and page down, and turned and walked quietly out of the room.

That was better than I could ever have hoped for, I thought.

But I was wrong. It turned out to be far worse than I could have dreaded. Because for the next number of days he did not say a word to me. I became invisible to him.

The strain grew and affected the household. After a week my mum said, "Kenneth, I think you need to clear the air with your dad," and I knew she was right. The atmosphere was awful.

I picked my time carefully. My father kept dozens of wild birds (he shouldn't have, but he did) in a simple aviary that he had put together in our backyard, and once a week the floor of the aviary needed brushing out. When my father was safely locked inside the aviary with brush in hand, I cautiously entered the backyard and stood alongside him.

For a few moments I did not know what to say, and the tension mounted. He started to brush the aviary floor more and more aggressively. Finally I stammered, "Dad, I'm sorry I failed the exam."

At first there was no reaction, but suddenly there was an explosion as his disappointment and pain came to the surface. He threw the brush down and turned to me, struggling at first to find the words to fit the pain.

"You'll never be able to get a decent job! You'll never be able to own a house or support a family!" he shouted. In his world this had proved to be true, and what he was really saying was that I would end up with the same major struggles that he had been contending with all his life. The emotional balloon had finally burst, however, and within hours it was over and normal life began to emerge once more.

But the damage was done. I understood that I would be a failure. My father had said so, and the exam result supported that declaration. The rest of my time at school merely reinforced this understanding.

It turned out that my Junior exam was the last Junior ever. The new GCSE qualification was introduced, which you sat when you were aged fifteen. So not only did I have to sit the last year of the Junior exam but the following year I also had to sit the first year of the GCSE exam.

It was a much fairer system: if you passed six subjects you got six GCSEs. Sadly, I could pass only English comprehension, written English, and oral English. Oh yes, and art. I was put into a new class called Fifth Lower Repeat for the failures who were being asked to re-sit the GCSE the following year. I gave up at that point and behaved badly, ending up on report for bad behavior, and at the exams could not improve on the first attempt.

Then school was over. At last. I left school with GCSE English and art, and a bad stammer. A failure in my father's eyes, my teachers' eyes, and of course, in my own eyes.

I began work as a waiter during the summer season on the Isle of Man, followed by two weeks as a trainee in a shoe factory in Ballymena, followed by six months in a Belfast fishing-tackle shop, before finally becoming a message boy with a scooter for a large regional newspaper called the *Belfast Telegraph*.

Here, however, things changed. I became driven by the sense of impending failure and started to work harder, go the extra mile, and dress better in order to get noticed. And get noticed I did. I became quite popular with the people in management. Not wanting to be a message boy all my life, I gingerly asked the classified sales manager if I could possibly train for telephone sales.

"No," he said. "And for four very good reasons. One, tele-ad sales staff must be female. Two, all tele-ad sales staff must be over twenty-one. Three, all tele-ad staff must be able to type. And four, all tele-ad staff must be able to speak clearly."

Of course I could see the problems. I was male, I was nineteen, I could not type, and I had a disabling stammer on most of my words. My head dropped. I said that I understood, and that I would have to leave soon, because I just could not be a message boy all my life.

At that, *his* head dropped somewhat. He liked me – all the managers did – and he clearly did not want me to leave, even though I was on the lowest rung.

"Look," he said, "to show you how ridiculous it would be, do two weeks face to face on advertising sales at the front desk."

I jumped at his suggestion, and this changed my life. Forever. I did very well, much better than the trained salesgirls who sat alongside me at the front desk. After much inter-management debate with Thomson Newspapers in London, a momentous decision was taken: I, a young lad of nineteen, would be given the standard two-week intense tele-ad training course and then be allowed to try telephone sales alongside some twenty gifted, older, female sales staff. I would be the first Thomson Group tele-ad boy.

I had to learn to type fast with two fingers. Had to battle with my ever-present stammer. Had two nervous breakdowns along the way. But amazingly, I slowly but surely made it up the corporate ladder to be the youngest outside sales rep, and the youngest person ever to get a company car (a red Mini). After six years surviving this pressure pot, I responded to a job ad placed by an advertising agency. We worked in lowly newspaper sales, but agencies were the glamorous side of advertising: multi-million-pound clients, television, radio, posters, and press.

I found the interview questions easy and got the job. Only afterwards did I realize why: I was a complete natural at creative thinking and writing (remember the exam passes in English and art). I was now an advertising executive.

Here I thrived. I loved every minute of this new world, and by my early thirties I became the joint owner of an advertising agency and the winner of a whole range of UK national, all-Ireland, and regional awards. My business partner and I had truly succeeded in our arena. And we kept on succeeding. We opened another communications business (public relations) and then another (design), and then another (sales marketing). We owned not only several businesses, but also 10,000 square feet of prime commercial property in the heart of Belfast.

Sport was no different. I was hugely competitive. I had to prove to myself, and to anyone who cared to look or listen, that I was not a failure. I did two New York marathons, eight Belfast marathons, one Dublin marathon, plus hundreds of smaller events. I did winter mountaineering in the Irish and Scottish mountains. I did rock climbing, sub aqua diving, parascending, parachuting, martial arts, and triathlons – finally ending up in the Triathlon World Championships at Nice in France in 1987. (But more about that event later on.)

My first wife, Anne, had tragically died of cancer at the age of twenty-three, leaving me with an eighteen-month-old son (now in his late thirties). I married Linda when I was thirty-one and we had three more beautiful children. We did all the sports together.

I drove a company Porsche, Linda a company Volvo Estate. What was it that drove me onwards and upwards?

Money? No, I had little interest in being wealthy.

Power? No, despite being labeled Managing Director and Creative Director.

Ambition? To some extent, perhaps. But this new lifestyle was all a bit of a shock to me really.

What drove me on and on was the internal understanding that my true identity was to be a failure. All along the way, I was expecting the monster called Failure to finally overtake me. I kept running harder and harder so that I could stay ahead of it for another few months. I was not running towards something; I was running away from something. On the surface I was a success, and outwardly I behaved as if I really was. I over-compensated for my inner fear of failure by always appearing extremely confident, even arrogant.

Then, at the age of forty-two, I became a Christian.

In fact Linda and I both became Christians at the same moment: on the last day of a Methodist holiday week held in Castlewellan Forest Park. When Rob Frost, the well-known evangelist, gave an altar call, we both rose immediately to our feet and went forward. It turned out that Linda had been thinking of doing this for nearly a year. My response was completely instinctive; I just knew that I was to make that move.

Linda had been raised as a Roman Catholic, but after we married, some ten years earlier, we had both begun to attend a small local Methodist church together. I had been brought up by Christian parents, and always believed in Jesus and His work at Calvary. I had said prayers every night since the age of three. My wife and I attended church every Sunday, hosted a cell group in our home every fortnight, and took Communion. Yet Jesus was not the Lord of our lives. We acknowledged Him, but we did not submit ourselves to Him. Until that August morning at Castlewellan Forest Park.

That day, kneeling at the front of the tent, submitting our lives to Jesus, we were both wonderfully "born again." We had heard that term used but had no understanding of what it meant. Now we knew. Jesus Christ became very real to us. The Bible came alive and we would often read it together until the early hours of the morning. We loved going to church and we loved the praise and worship. We even looked for midweek events that we could attend in other churches. The hunger was insatiable.

I could not help but tell every employee in work, every client, and every neighbor, about the sheer reality of Jesus Christ. Two members of my local running club, after hearing the story of our conversion the previous week, asked if they could come to church with us on Sunday. There they too went to the front and gave their lives to Jesus.

Every evening, we would visit friends and family to evangelize with a passion. Our unabated enthusiasm was either terrifying or infectious. (I suspect that for many it was the former.) The minister of our Methodist church even mentioned us on the radio during one of the "God slots" on early morning local radio.

Then six months later an event occurred which threw me into what is sometimes called "the dark night of the soul." This is not the book to teach into this subject, but it is a reality. When God chooses to use a man or woman in a special way, He often leads them into a difficult place in order to shape them for their particular calling. Think of Moses; think of Joseph. Sometimes Satan is given permission to aggressively confront or even sift a person as part of God's plans and purposes. Think of Jesus being led by the Holy Spirit into the wilderness for forty days to be confronted by Satan before being released into His ministry.[1] Think of Peter being sifted[2] and how it changed him before he could be released into his ministry.[3]

To sum up my dark night of the soul, I became totally tormented, night and day, with ferocious fears in my mind and obscene demonic images continually flashing before my eyes. This relentless round-the-clock torment quickly wore me down. I had to leave both home and work for a period of time, and went to stay with my mum (my father had died some years earlier). She patiently and lovingly sat with me at all hours of the day and night, comforting me. This "dark night" lasted for almost a full year, until ten past six on the evening of 27 December 1991 when, with one touch from Jesus, I was completely set free.

My calling and my ministry journey started just three months later, and has continued now for nearly two decades. The person that I became was the fruit of that dreadful year.

Throughout that period, my wife took me to many churches to see if they could help me, but none could. We still attended the Methodist fellowship, but I can remember her taking me also to Pentecostal, Baptist, and Assemblies of God churches. I quickly realized that the standard church minister or pastor has no understanding or training in such areas of spiritual experience; and this, I believe, was part of what God wanted me to see.

At the nine-month stage of this awful journey we appealed again to our own Methodist minister. He made some phone calls and said that he had arranged for a group of men "who knew about these things" to come to our home and minister to me.

They duly arrived, and certainly they did know more than the people we had encountered over the previous months. I believe that under normal circumstances their ministry would have set me free, but as this proved to be a God-ordained journey, I was not to be set free until whatever God wanted done in me was done. That day would come three months later.

However, this is the point I am building up to: While the men were in our home, I vividly remember these few moments that I will now describe.

The oldest of the men walked over to stand behind our sofa, and said to me, "Kenneth, don't you know that even if you were to lie down on this sofa for a year, your Heavenly Father would still love you?"

I had two reactions to this question. I heard my mouth giving him the theologically correct, official Christian answer: "Oh yes, I know that." But inside me there was an invisible explosion of what was almost rage, in which I was silently screaming at him, saying, "You fool, you stupid fool! You and I both know that if I was to lie on that sofa and do nothing for a year, my Heavenly Father would turn His back on me and not speak to me!" That was my hidden but very real perception of my Heavenly Father.

Let's stop for a few moments and reflect.

When, for the first six months after my conversion, I was deemed by myself to be a successful Christian, I genuinely believed that God the Father would love me and indeed be proud of me. Now, because of the relentless torment that had engulfed me, I was, in my eyes, a useless Christian, a public embarrassment to God, a burden to my wife and family and to the church. I believed that God the Father would be greatly disappointed with me and would turn His back to me.

Thinking back over my experiences with my father, why do you think I perceived God the Father in this way?

Notes

1. Luke 4:1, 14.
2. Luke 22:31.
3. John 21:15–17.

CHAPTER 3

MY JOURNEY BEGINS

The fact that I have been teaching this subject for more than a decade in many parts of the world, and have written this book on the subject, shows that I have come a long way from that starting point. What happened?

Several things, clearly orchestrated by God Himself, brought Light into the darkness of my misunderstanding. Let me share them with you.

My youngest son, David, never ate his lunch when he was at primary school, and as parents we were concerned about that. So every day when he got home from school, Linda would check through the little school bag to see if he had eaten anything. One day as she looked through his lunchbox, she found a short essay on a sheet of paper with the title, "My Dad."

Now this is where primary school teachers must get telling insights into their young pupils' home life. Young children, in their innocence, tell things as they are. They haven't yet been coached with the family public relations spin! So I knew that whatever I was about to read would be "the truth."

Below is David's short essay, as it was written, spelling mistakes and all.

To help you make sense of it, I need to fill in a few background details. My job, as already mentioned, was at that time in advertising. (That's a big word to spell when you are only eight years of age.) Occasionally, I was asked to speak at the Presbyterian church we attended for many years. We used to holiday every year at a place in the west of Ireland known as "the Burren" where the main tourist attraction is a cave, only discovered in 1956; and because several bones of the now-extinct Irish bear were found inside, it became known as "the Bear's Cave." Visitors could buy fossils at the coffee and craft shop attached to the Bear's Cave. And of course, as you know, my hobby at the time was fishing.

Now you are ready to read!

David 22nd June 1995

My Dad

My Dad is called ken Symington he is an andfortiser but mostly he pelps in church and some times he takes it himself. he takes my brother stephen and me. He always takes us to the burn there is a bears cave up in a hill that you can walk inside it you can find good fosalies there. I think my dads best hoppy is fishing . . .

So far, it's fairly factual, with nothing particularly noteworthy. But there is one line left. And that line had a profound effect on me:

. . . He is a good dad to me and I love him.

When you're raising children, you are acutely aware of your many failings. If you are a caring parent you know what I mean: "Maybe I'm not spending enough time with them. Maybe I'm too involved in business or sport. Maybe I should help them more with their homework," and so on. The truth is that until you see the need to change, you usually just pass on the type of parenting you received.

Yet David had written – and amazingly the teacher had *read* – that I was a good dad to him and that he loved me.

This simple line, obviously the truth to David, was worth a million pounds to me. As a result, everywhere I went I took this "essay" with me. Because I was the boss at work and had meetings with clients every day, I had many opportunities to show off this essay to anyone and everyone. I would skillfully bring every conversation round to the government, then on to the education system, and then, "By the way, have you read what my son wrote at school . . ."

Everyone had to read this. I only stopped when, after a month, on a train to Dublin sitting opposite a business colleague, I offered him the chance to read it as well. The look he gave me made me realize I was becoming somewhat obsessive. After that I took the page home, framed it, and put it – pride of place – in my office at home.

A few weeks later, while driving the car to work, I felt God speak into my spirit. I'm not talking about an audible voice (though that has happened to me once) but a sudden encounter of God's Spirit witnessing with my spirit, and then my mind unpacking it line by line. This is my best way of describing the encounter.

God asked, "What did you think of your son's essay?"

(By the way, when God asks a question it's not that He doesn't know the answer. He asks so that He can draw your attention to the matter. Remember "Adam, where are you?"[1] "Moses, what is that in your hand?"[2])

I replied, "Lord, you know what I think about it. It really blessed me."

God continued, "How many marks out of 10 would you give it for English grammar and punctuation?"

"Well, he's only eight years old. I'd probably give him 4 or 5 out of 10 for effort," I answered.

God said, "Did that in any way diminish it?"

"No," I replied. "I think it might even have added to it, as it showed that he still needed me."

God then asked, "What was your favorite line?"

It was of course the line, "He's a good dad to me and I love him."

To my shock, I then felt Father God say to me, "Could you say that to *me*?"

To this day I can remember where I was when that happened. The God who created the universe, the Sovereign Lord of everything in heaven, in earth, and under the earth, was apparently asking if I could say to Him, "You are a good Dad to me and I love you."

It seemed ridiculous to my logical mind, but as God initiated it I thought I had better do it anyway. So, bracing myself, and indeed feeling somewhat ridiculous, I said out loud inside the car, "You're a good Dad to me and I love you."

As soon as I said that, I felt something really nice happen deep inside me. For days on end I just kept saying it over and over again: "You're a good Dad to me and I love you!" What started as a duty gradually became a joy, because as I said those words, something good was definitely happening. With hindsight, I now believe that I was sensing God's pleasure. My spirit was picking up my Father God's delight!

It was then, for the first time, that I began to understand that when God calls Himself "Father" it is not just a "title" but also a perfect description of His character. God could call Himself "The Great Dictator of the Universe," and who could deny Him that? In fact He could give Himself any title He wanted.

But He calls Himself "Father" because, from the beginning of creation, that has been His heart.[3] Scripture is simply awash with confirming terms, such as newborn babies,[4] children,[5] sons and daughters,[6] firstborn,[7] family in heaven and earth.[8] He truly wants to father us with great love. Imagine that – with great love!

> How great is the love the Father has lavished on us, that we should be called children of God! And that is what we are! The reason the world does not know us is that it did not know him.
>
> (1 John 3:1)

I had never seen Father God in that way before. I had always seen Him as someone busy analyzing my every moment in life, probably keeping a score of all my mistakes. I knew I was going to heaven all right, because of what Jesus had done on the cross. Jesus was my Lord and my Savior; Jesus was my Friend, and I could count on Him to ensure that I got there safely. But God the Father was, well, not so attractive. He wasn't quite so friendly – not the way Jesus was.

As I continued along this new line of thinking about God "the Father," and reading my Bible through these new glasses, things began to become clear. God hadn't sent Jesus to bring people to Jesus. God sent Jesus to bring people back to *Him*, their Father. God the Father was the great prize.

> Jesus answered, "I am the way and the truth and the life. No-one comes to the Father except through me."
>
> (John 14:6)

Yes, God the Father was the Great Prize! Not the great dread!

Yet for so long I had missed that. Oh yes, through Jesus I had God the Father "in position," but not in a day-to-day, living relationship. I had never crossed the bridge from Jesus to seek and encounter the One who sent Him. But I was beginning to see it now. Jesus rescued me, saved me, and I was saved totally and completely. But it was Jesus Himself who said that I could never have come to Him in the first place unless God the Father – His Father – had drawn me to Him.

> No one can come to Me unless the Father who sent Me draws him . . .
>
> (John 6:44a NKJV)

> And He [Jesus] said, "Therefore I have said to you that no one can come to Me unless it has been granted to him by My Father."
>
> (John 6:65 NKJV)

Can you see it as I was beginning to see it? I was not forced upon God the Father when Jesus saved me. God the Father actually wanted me! He set the wheels in motion in heaven, and Jesus outworked His will perfectly here on earth. He wanted me in His family. He was willing for His only begotten Son to suffer death on a cross to make a way for me to come home to Him – to come into a real Father/son relationship with Him. Forever.

And guess what? He wanted you too. When Jesus saved you, He was outworking the will of His Father. God the Father wants you to come into a real Father/son or Father/daughter relationship with Him. Forever. Jesus came and made the way for that to happen.

God the Father wants us, His children, to know him in a day-by-day, living experience as well as in a sound theological position. God wants us to have more than just head-knowledge of Him; He wants us to have a heart-to-heart relationship. Jesus Himself prayed the night before He was arrested,

> Now this is eternal life: that they may know you, the only true God, and Jesus Christ, whom you have sent.
>
> (John 17:3)

Let us pause here a while and reflect.

Do you understand the amazing transaction that took place at the crucifixion?

If you truly believed that you were God the Father's *much-wanted, much-loved, and much-cherished child*, how different might your life be?

Notes

1. Genesis 3:9.
2. Exodus 4:2.
3. Luke 3:38.
4. 1 Peter 2:2.
5. John 1:12.
6. 2 Corinthians 6:18.
7. Exodus 4:22.
8. Ephesians 3:15.

CHAPTER 4

SEEING THE FATHER'S HEART

When God wanted to reveal truth to astronomers, He sent a star.[1] If you are a musician He may reveal truth to you through music. If you are a mathematician He may reveal truth to you through mathematics.

I love the great outdoors. My father used to take me for a walk most Sundays after church and show me the wonders of nature in the fields, woodlands, and rivers near our home. He could identify most birds by their song, or their style of flight. Whereas most people might be able to identify sparrows, blackbirds, robins, chaffinches, and pigeons, I, from an early age, was able to identify red linnets, hawfinches, bullfinches, greenfinches, yellowhammers, linnets, sparrowhawks, coal tits, and the like.

Most Sundays, we would get an old discarded wicker basket from a nearby rubbish dump (for common rubbish fifty-five years ago) and use the basket to block up a small stream called the Gudgeon Stream, which ran down a gentle slope into the River Lagan. With the basket now acting as a net, my father would get a long stick and, starting maybe 10 meters upstream, he would walk towards the basket, agitating the reeds and water with his stick. The idea was to chase all river life ahead of him until it reached the basket. When the stream was well muddied from this disturbance, he would carefully lift the basket out, wait until the water had drained out through the wicker strands, and then look in the mud for all the various life forms.

Thus I grew up familiar with sticklebacks, tadpoles and frogs, leeches, eels, gudgeon, great diving beetles, dragonfly larvae, and the like.

We lived in a mid-terrace house, and it seemed as though we always had unusual pets in our long whitewashed backyard. We had a pet jackdaw for twenty-seven years who, not surprisingly, was called Jackie. He could mimic my father's laugh perfectly. He was a fierce bird who believed that we should be frightened of him, and took a delight in pretending to be tame by putting his head down and leaning towards you as if wanting to be stroked, only to turn, with a raucous laugh, and attack the approaching hand. Thus we often had fun with visitors to our home.

When I was very young, I remember a baby fox running up and down our backyard. At one stage my father kept an owl.

You get the picture! This continual interaction with nature touched a chord deep within me, and as I grew older, my love for the outdoors and for nature increased. I loved walking and climbing in the mountains, and sleeping out overnight under a rock. I loved the seas and for many years was an enthusiastic sub aqua diver.

So, with hindsight, I see why God began to reveal Himself and His heart to me through "the things that are made."[2]

This is of course very scriptural. Paul wrote:

> For since the creation of the world God's invisible qualities – his eternal power and divine nature – have been clearly seen, being understood from what has been made . . .
>
> (Romans 1:20a)

The things that are made reveal the Father heart of God so powerfully that Paul completed his sentence by adding,

. . . so that men are without excuse.

(Romans 1:20b)

What Paul was saying is this: The same Personality that made the invisible but very real spiritual realm also made the visible physical realm that we interact with daily. When art experts get to know the style of Picasso or Rembrandt, they can recognize their works no matter what subject they chose to paint. The artist's personality comes through all his creations. Therefore, despite the fact that this is a fallen world,[3] you can still, by looking closely at the things that are made, get a good picture of the Personality and Character of the One who made both the physical and the spiritual realm.

That's why Jesus taught Kingdom truth from the everyday created things that were all around Him. He used sheep, goats, and lambs, vines and fig trees, seeds and harvest, wheat and chaff, oil and wine, sand and rocks, sunsets and rain, wind and streams, sparrows and eagles, to reveal truth.

Here's a sample. Picture Jesus standing next to a vine in one of the thousands of vineyards that would have dotted the hillsides of Israel. Everyone listening knew about tending vines. Now imagine yourself standing among the listeners as Jesus points to the nearest vine and starts teaching about the Kingdom of God.

> I am the true vine, and my Father is the gardener. He cuts off every branch in me that bears no fruit, while every branch that does bear fruit he prunes so that it will be even more fruitful. You are already clean because of the word I have spoken to you.
>
> (John 15:1–3)

Maybe He stopped and broke a branch off before continuing:

> Remain in me, and I will remain in you. No branch can bear fruit by itself; it must remain in the vine. Neither can you bear fruit unless you remain in me.

I am the vine; you are the branches. If a man remains in me and
I in him, he will bear much fruit; apart from me you can do nothing.

(John 15:4–5)

I can understand that truth, and so can you. The natural is a teaching
aid to help us grasp the spiritual. Paul wrote:

However, the spiritual is not first, but the natural, and afterward
the spiritual.

(1 Corinthians 15:46 NKJV)

Now you can see why the "god of this age" relentlessly continues to
proclaim that the world around us made itself by random unguided
events that turned out well. He blinds the eyes to the glorious truth
that is all around us.[4]

Before we move on to the positive, let me quickly deal with the
attacks on the truth that God created the world around us. The
aggressively proclaimed "molecules to man" upward evolution is a
hypothesis,[5] not a fact. In the last 200 years there have been more than
100 billion fossils found, and Dr Michael Denton MD PhD (molecular
biologist at the University of Otago, New Zealand) in his book
Evolution: A Theory in Crisis states that this covers 97.7% of living
orders of land vertebrates. Yet even with such a vast sample to work
with, not even one clear transitional fossil trail has been found.

Charles Darwin, in his book *The Origin of Species*, acknowledged
this problem:

*The number of intermediate varieties which have formerly
existed on earth must be truly enormous. Why is not every
geological formation and every stratum full of such
intermediate links? Geology assuredly does not reveal any such
finely graduated organic chain; and this is the most obvious
and serious objection which can be urged against my theory.*[6]

Micro-evolution, which would probably be better termed as "speciation" (development within a kind) is a fact, but macro-evolution (development upwards from one kind into another kind) is not. This simply means that fish, dogs, cats, birds, moths etc. may change in color, size, shape, and behavior as breeding, feeding, and circumstances shape them, but never has it been proved that they have evolved upwards *through added genetic information* into another "kind." That part is the "theory" still waiting for proof.

In Darwin's day a simple cell was thought of as something akin to a blob of protoplasm, and the understanding was that, given enough time, random mutations that proved advantageous could slowly but surely change a life form upwards into a whole new life form. Modern science now shows that a "simple" cell is more complex than a major city, and the discovery of DNA – which provides the blueprint for all life forms – has changed the views of many. If the information in even a pinhead of DNA was written into paperback books like this one, the information would fill enough books to reach to the moon 500 times.[7] The growing understanding is that there could be no changes upwards unless there was added genetic information, and there is no known process by which this can be achieved.

Dr Werner Gitt, an information scientist, says, "There is no known natural law through which matter can give rise to information, neither is any physical process or material phenomenon known that can do this." He also points out that "there is no known law of nature, no known process, no known sequence of events, which can cause information to originate, by itself, in matter."[8]

The theory that mutations could add information has never been proved. Rather, the opposite has happened. Dr Lee Spetner, a physicist and formerly a fellow at Johns Hopkins University, states: "All point mutations that have been studied on a molecular level turn out to reduce the genetic information and not to increase it." He emphasizes this by saying:

... not even one mutation has been observed that adds a little information to the genome. That surely shows that there are not the millions upon millions of potential mutations the theory demands. There may well not be any. The failure to observe even one mutation that adds information is more than just a failure to find support for the theory. It is evidence against the theory. We have here a serious challenge to neo-Darwinian theory.[9]

The most renowned scientist to "change his mind" because of these new discoveries and improved understanding is undoubtedly British philosopher Antony Flew. For more than fifty years he was the world's most aggressive atheist, writing many books and leaflets against religious faith and, debating publicly many times with theologians and pastors in front of enormous crowds. Then in 2004 he changed his position from that of atheist to theist, because that is where the information led him. He wrote:

I must say again that the journey to my discovery of the Divine has thus far been a pilgrimage of reason. I have followed the argument where it led me. And it has led me to accept the existence of a self-existent, immutable, immaterial, omnipotent, and omniscient Being.[10]

In 2006 he added his name to a petition calling for intelligent Design to be taught in schools.

Despite billions spent in research trying to discover how "life" came into being, it remains, to this day, a mystery to those who reject the clear teaching in the Bible. In an interview with Benjamin Wiker, Professor Flew said:

With every passing year, the more that was discovered about the richness and inherent intelligence of life, the less it seemed likely that a chemical soup could magically generate the genetic code. The difference between life and non-life, it became apparent to me, was ontological and not chemical. The best confirmation of this radical gulf is Richard Dawkins' comical effort to argue in The God Delusion *that the origin of life can be attributed to a "lucky chance." If that's the best argument you have, then the game is over. No, I did not hear a Voice. It was the evidence itself that led me to this conclusion.*[11]

So, to sum up before we move on, we can say that God created life to be able to adapt to changing circumstances and thus, as we witness all around us, it can develop endlessly sideways, but never upwards with increasing complexity. (If you want to pursue this, I recommend spending quality time on one of the dedicated Christian creation websites such as Answers in Genesis, Creation Ministries International, Creation on the Web, and the Institute for Creation Research.)

Now onwards on this adventure, as I show you what God showed me.

Let's start with the miracle of the sun. Although this ball of hydrogen and helium gas "burns" through continual nuclear reactions at its core, its trinity of energy, light, and heat never goes out. Sometimes it even flares up.

Planet earth journeys around this sun once a year at an average distance of 93 million miles and at a speed of about 66,000 mph. If earth was just 5% closer to the sun, the oceans would boil and the waters evaporate. If it were just 5% further away, the oceans would freeze.

Then there's the miracle of the vast and mighty oceans. If the oceans were half their size, we would get only 25% of our present rainfall. If the oceans were only one-eighth larger, then annual rainfall would increase by 400%, turning this planet of ours into an uninhabitable swamp. Water solidifies at 0 degrees Celsius, but if earth's oceans were subject to that law, the amount of thawing in the polar regions wouldn't balance out and everything would end up encased in ice. Amazingly, the oceans have salt in them to prevent this catastrophe. Even the largest inland lakes on earth have no such salt levels.

So perfect is all this, that the most northerly and southerly parts of planet earth are too cold to sustain any reasonable level of existence, while by contrast, the most central part of earth is too hot to sustain any reasonable level of existence. Most of us live in the temperate regions situated between the two extremes.

At the equator, earth spins at close to 1,000 mph as it travels on its 365-day journey around the sun, giving us day and night. Otherwise one side would have permanent light and the other side permanent darkness, and nothing could grow. If the earth's rotation was much slower than it is, our days would be unbearably hot and our nights freezing cold. All the while, this amazing planet that we call earth is tilted at 23.5 degrees – to give us seasons. And all the while, its north "pole" is always pointed at the pole star (Polaris).

The moon revolves around our planet once a month, at a distance of some 240,000 miles, ensuring – with its gravitational pull – that the vast oceans on this planet have twice-daily tides replenishing them with oxygen, thus allowing fish to breathe. The moon's size, and thus its gravitational pull, in tandem with its distance from the earth, slows the earth's spin down to the livable speed that permits life to exist.

Interestingly, the earth's distance from the sun is 400 times the earth's distance from the moon, and the sun is 400 times the diameter of the moon. This means that the sun and moon appear to be about the same size when viewed from the earth. This remarkable "coincidence" enables us occasionally to view a total eclipse of the sun. That wouldn't be possible if the moon wasn't exactly the size it is.

The very large planet called Jupiter is superbly positioned as a sort of meteorite vacuum cleaner. It has even been termed "the great protector." Its strong gravitational pull draws meteorites towards itself that would otherwise potentially damage or even destroy the earth.

Then there's earth's own gravitational pull. If this planet were significantly smaller, the lessened gravity would not be capable of holding the atmosphere that is essential for breathing. A much thinner atmosphere would provide no protection from the 25,000 meteors that burn up in the atmosphere over this planet every day. If the planet was twice as large, the effect of increased gravity would make everything on earth's surface weigh eight times what it weighs today.

Truly "the heavens declare the glory of God; the skies proclaim the work of his hands."[12]

Professor Robert Jastrow, in *The Intellectuals Speak Out About God*, says,

> *The smallest change in any of the circumstances of the natural world, such as the relative strengths of the forces of nature, or the properties of the elementary particles, would have led to a universe in which there could be no life and no man. For example, if nuclear forces were decreased by a few percent, the particles of the universe would not have come together in nuclear reactions to make the ingredients, such as carbon atoms, of which life must be constructed.*[13]

Now let's look more closely at planet earth itself. And imagine some of the choices that your Heavenly Father might have faced.

He could choose to fill the seas with just one species of fish – let's say, mackerel. They look good, taste good, and are very easy to catch. That would be amazing. Or He could choose the extravagant option and fill the seas with dolphins, whales, John Dorys, cod, halibut, marlin, wrasse, moray eels, manta ray and . . . Well, you get the idea. How extravagant is extravagant? There are 1,500 species of fish, including thirty species of whales, dolphins, and porpoises that live in, or visit, the Great Barrier Reef alone. Then there are the freshwater species that live in rivers and lakes, which make up more than 40% of the total number of fish species. The numbers are simply staggering. That's extravagant. From a very extravagant Personality.

Another choice might have been to fill the earth with just one species of animal – let's say, rabbits. They're cuddly and cute, taste good, and breed, well, like rabbits. Or choose the extravagant option and fill the earth with lions and tigers, horses, camels, dogs and cats, elephants, buffalo, giraffes, sheep and cows, wildebeest, anteaters, monkeys and . . . Well, again, you get the idea.

How extravagant is extravagant? There are 167 species of animals living in Africa alone, including five of the world's six fastest. That's before you even think about Australia, Asia, and the Americas. That's extravagant. From a very extravagant Personality.

Another choice might have been whether to bless the earth with one species of bird – let's say, sparrows. (God seems to like the humble sparrow since Jesus singled it out for mention in one of His teachings.[14]) Or choose the extravagant option and fill the earth with pelicans, eagles, canaries, ducks, ospreys, hummingbirds, swans, finches, rainbow lorikeets, king parrots, peacocks and . . .

How extravagant is extravagant? There are almost 9,000 species of birds populating the skies above us. That's extravagant. From a very extravagant Personality.

Another choice might have been whether to bless the earth with one species of tree – let's say, the magnificent oak. Tall, strong, and superb for building with. Or (and yes, you're with me by now) choose the extravagant option again and fill the earth with orange and apple trees, silver birch, Portuguese variegated laurel, gum, giant redwood, bristle brush pine and so on and so on and so on.

How extravagant is extravagant? There are an estimated 100,000 species of trees planted into this planet we call home. That's extravagant. From a very extravagant Personality.

Where do we stop? Let's go on with butterflies. There are more than 17,500 species of butterfly on planet earth. They begin life as slow, earthbound caterpillars. Then they turn into a coffin-like chrysalis, before finally breaking free and fluttering heavenwards as delicate, beautiful, colorful flying miracles.

Imagine now if God had taken the ungenerous option. We would still be blessed because we wouldn't know what we might be missing. But He showed His generous, extravagant Personality in the heavens, the skies, the earth, and the seas.

He is not mean. He is extravagantly generous. And colorful. He could have created all flowers to be a nice shade of yellow. And we would be blessed. But He chose extravagance. There are an estimated quarter of a million different flowering plants!

He could have let all food taste like bread. But he chose extravagance. Imagine life without tomatoes, bananas, potatoes, leeks, carrots, apples and oranges. Imagine life without garlic, chili, sugar, lemon, thyme, salt and pepper. There are more than 10,000 different herbs in the world.

Or imagine the thousands of flavors and textures but no sensitive taste buds to enjoy them. Our tongues have around 10,000 taste buds! Imagine no eyes to see the flowers, the sunrises and sunsets. No ears to hear the birdsong.

We could go on all day! God's Personality is truly revealed as generous and extravagant. All this declares His glory. As the Bible says, "the whole earth is full of his glory."[15]

But the biggest surprise is yet to be revealed. Fasten your seatbelts . . .

With all its extravagant interlinking glory, this is not heaven. (Heaven is of course unimaginably better.) This planet was made for us. The light, the land, the grass, the trees, the stars, the fish, the birds, and the land creatures were created with the spoken word.[16] When all was in place, we read of the amazing conversation within the Godhead.

> Then God said, "Let us make man in our image, in our likeness . . ."
>
> (Genesis 1:26a)

He took up some dust from the earth and did not fashion it into a monkey, but into His own image. He wanted children. Adam, son of God,[17] go forth and multiply.[18] More children, please.

God did not ask "mother earth" to breathe life into His offspring. Nor did He ask the archangels Michael or Gabriel to breathe life into His offspring. He breathed His life into the first Adam, and the human race was alive, and – at that time – alive unto God.[19]

Let me tell you a story to help you grasp what this chapter means.

When our first baby was expected, we turned the spare bedroom into a nursery for this much-wanted child. We didn't have much money, but we bought the best we could afford. Soft underlay under a colorful carpet. Baby wallpaper with matching curtains and lightshade. A set of white drawers with a nice changing-mat on top. A safe cot and mattress. Colorful toys on the floor. Cartoon characters in pictures on the walls. When guests were shown the room, they could clearly see how much this child was wanted.

If money had been no object and the room that people were shown had bare walls and floorboards, a bare light bulb, and a box and newspapers for a crib, then it would be safe to say the guests would have understood that the coming baby was of little interest and of little value to us.

Here's the bombshell: This amazing, extravagant, colorful, perfectly tuned planet was not a cosmic accident. This was the nursery. The nursery for what was really on God's heart.

The nursery was for us. For you and me.

Now put the book down for a moment and reflect.

Do you understand that God the Father wanted "children"?

Do you understand that He wanted you?

Notes

1. Matthew 2:9.
2. Romans 1:20 NKJV.
3. Romans 8:22.
4. 2 Corinthians 4:4.
5. Hypothesis – a supposition or proposed explanation made on the basis of limited evidence as a starting point for further investigation.
5. Charles Darwin, *The Origin of Species* (Penguin, 1968), p. 291.
7. http://www.answersingenesis.org/creation/v20/i1/design.asp.
8. Dr Werner Gitt, *In the Beginning Was Information* (CLV, 1997), pp. 64–67.
9. Dr Lee Spetner, *Not By Chance: Shattering the Modern Idea of Evolution* (The Judaica Press, 1997), pp. 159–160).
10. Antony Flew and Roy A. Varghese, *There Is a God: How the World's Most Notorious Atheist Changed His Mind* (HarperOne, 2007), p. 155.
11. http://iesvs.tripod.com/FLEW.htm.
12. Psalm 19:1.
13. Dr Robert Jastrow, *The Intellectuals Speak Out About God* (Regnery Gateway, 1984), p. 21.
14. Matthew 10:31.
15. Isaiah 6:3.
16. Genesis 1:1–24.
17. Luke 3:38.
18. Genesis 1:28.
19. Genesis 2:7.

CHAPTER 5

THE FATHER'S
WOUNDED HEART

If you are a parent you will understand this short chapter.

You love your child. You devote nearly all your time and effort towards their well-being. Your plans for them are only good. You want only the best for them. You want them to prosper and to have good character. To have integrity. You try not to show it, but you are blessed when someone says to your child, "You are just like your mum [or dad]."

There is nothing you would not do for them. You would lay down your life for them. You know what is best for them, what is safe for them. When they are young, they listen to you. When you say, "Don't play in the middle of the road," they obey. You put safe boundaries around them.

Then comes the day when they rebel. They go their own way. Perhaps wrong friends. Perhaps wrong films, or violent computer games. Perhaps drugs. Perhaps alcohol. Or all of these.

They show no respect for you or any other authority figure, while always demanding respect for themselves. You see in them a growing pull towards darkness, and a distaste for what is right. Childhood prayers are no more, replaced by an anti-God position. There is no

God. Christians are stupid people. You are no longer an influence. The world, especially the media, has been given that mantle.

If it were someone else's child you would be sad for them. But when it is your child, your heart is so grieved, your pain is so intense, so prolonged, that at times you almost wish you had not become a parent.

God the Father wanted only the best for His children.

> "For I know the plans I have for you," declares the LORD, "plans to prosper you and not to harm you, plans to give you hope and a future . . . "
>
> (Jeremiah 29:11)

This awesome nursery called planet earth was for His sons and daughters to subdue and enjoy and have adventure in and multiply in, but the one condition, the one safe boundary, was that He, their Heavenly Father, would decide what was good and what was evil.[1] That has never changed.

At first Adam and Eve walked and talked with God, presumably spirit to Spirit, in the garden in the cool of the afternoon.[2] Adam and Eve were obedient, they were covered, and they were safe. Life was good.

Then we know what happened.

The devil, that old serpent, evicted from heaven,[3] began to communicate with them. He spoke of God their Father as a cold, controlling authority figure who did not want the best for His children, and he advised them to go it alone without God. They could then decide what was good and what was evil, and they could be the god of their own lives.

> For God knows that when you eat of it your eyes will be opened, and you will be like God, knowing good and evil.
>
> (Genesis 3:5)

They listened, and they chose to reject God their Father. Slowly but surely, and now under the unseen but very real authority of the devil (sometimes called the "god of this age,"[4] the "ruler of the kingdom of the air,"[5] and the "prince of this world"[6]), they began to sink into immorality, family breakdown, violence, and defilement.

Rebellion hardened the heart and became pride, which became arrogance, which became jealousy, which became greed, and which eventually became murder. Here's a sample:

> Now Cain said to his brother Abel, "Let's go out to the field." And while they were in the field, Cain attacked his brother Abel and killed him.
>
> Then the LORD said to Cain, "Where is your brother Abel?"
>
> "I don't know," he replied. "Am I my brother's keeper?"
>
> (Genesis 4:8–9)

> Lamech said to his wives,

> "Adah and Zillah, listen to me;
>   wives of Lamech, hear my words.
> I have killed a man for wounding me,
>   a young man for injuring me.
> If Cain is avenged seven times,
>   then Lamech seventy-seven times."
>
> (Genesis 4:23–24)

We've reaching the end of this short chapter. *Time to reflect.*

God wanted the very best for His children, but they rebelled and went their own way. Maybe you've never thought of God the Father's heart being grieved by that. Ponder His pain in this verse:

> The LORD saw how great man's wickedness on the earth had become, and that every inclination of the thoughts of his heart was only evil

all the time. The LORD was grieved that he had made man on the earth, and his heart was filled with pain.

(Genesis 6:5–6)

Ponder that even with us, in the New Covenant, His heart can still be grieved when we continue to behave out of our old nature, because He wants the best for us.

And do not grieve the Holy Spirit of God, with whom you were sealed for the day of redemption. Get rid of all bitterness, rage and anger, brawling and slander, along with every form of malice.

(Ephesians 4:30–31)

We have emotions because we are made in God's image, and God has emotions. We read here of His grieved heart, which reveals a sensitive heart, but elsewhere we read of His joy,[7] His gladness, His love, His singing,[8] and yes, His anger.

In the next chapter we will look at His anger.

Notes

1. Genesis 2:16–17.
2. Genesis 3:8.
3. Isaiah 14:12–14.
4. 2 Corinthians 4:4.
5. Ephesians 2:2.
6. John 12:31.
7. Nehemiah 8:10.
8. Zephaniah 3:17.

CHAPTER 6

THE ANGRY FATHER

What makes you angry? I mean *really* angry. If you see or hear of cruelty to children, does that make you angry? I suspect it does. That is what the Bible calls a "righteous anger."

It made God angry when "His people" were sacrificing their children to the god Molech.[1] That's a righteous anger. Molech was a large cast-iron "god" who held out his hands to receive the children from their parents. When the children were placed into his grasp, they rolled down the hands and into a fire where they died an unimaginable death. How might God feel about the millions of babies aborted on the altar of convenience and lifestyle?

Would seeing a vulnerable widow or a fatherless child being mistreated by society make you angry? I suspect it would. It certainly made God the Father angry because they had no man to protect them.[2] I love this short, simple verse where the writer declares,

> Though my father and mother forsake me,
> the LORD will receive me.

> (Psalm 27:10)

Would people taking advantage of the poor make you angry? It should. It certainly made God the Father angry.[3]

Have you ever been in a foreign land and been mistreated because you were a foreigner? Would people mistreating the strangers in your country make you angry? It made God angry.[4]

When you see society being aggressively polluted by all sorts of sexual perversion, does it make you angry? It made God angry.[5] If you are a faithful spouse but your spouse is continually unfaithful to you, would that make you angry?

You get the picture.

Listen to Jesus reveal His Father's heart. It hasn't changed. I find this passage powerful, emotional, and a little scary (it's meant to be[6]), but I love my Father for standing up for the weakest in our world.

> When the Son of Man comes in his glory, and all the angels with him, he will sit on his throne in heavenly glory. All the nations will be gathered before him, and he will separate the people one from another as a shepherd separates the sheep from the goats. He will put the sheep on his right and the goats on his left.
>
> Then the King will say to those on his right, "Come, you who are blessed by my Father; take your inheritance, the kingdom prepared for you since the creation of the world. For I was hungry and you gave me something to eat, I was thirsty and you gave me something to drink, I was a stranger and you invited me in, I needed clothes and you clothed me, I was sick and you looked after me, I was in prison and you came to visit me."
>
> Then the righteous will answer him, "Lord, when did we see you hungry and feed you, or thirsty and give you something to drink? When did we see you a stranger and invite you in, or needing clothes and clothe you? When did we see you sick or in prison and go to visit you?"
>
> The King will reply, "I tell you the truth, whatever you did for one of the least of these brothers of mine, you did for me."

Then he will say to those on his left, "Depart from me, you who are cursed, into the eternal fire prepared for the devil and his angels. For I was hungry and you gave me nothing to eat, I was thirsty and you gave me nothing to drink, I was a stranger and you did not invite me in, I needed clothes and you did not clothe me, I was sick and in prison and you did not look after me."

They also will answer, "Lord, when did we see you hungry or thirsty or a stranger or needing clothes or sick or in prison, and did not help you?"

He will reply, "I tell you the truth, whatever you did not do for one of the least of these, you did not do for me."

Then they will go away to eternal punishment, but the righteous to eternal life.

(Matthew 25:31–46)

Can you begin to tune in to the Father's heart? To see His protective concern for the "least" of people. The weak. The poor. The sick. The naked and hungry. The downtrodden. The victim. The stranger. The prisoner. And His anger when they are abused or mistreated. Always, always a righteous anger. A righteous anger to be taken seriously.

God is not passive.

Wherever Jesus walked, whatever He did, and whatever He said, He was always outworking His Father's heart.[7] Remember the lepers? The blind? The deaf and dumb?[8] The sick and the demonized?[9] The hated tax-collectors?[10] The ritually unclean woman with the issue of blood whom society scorned?[11]

Remember the detested foreigners such as the Canaanite woman with the demonized daughter,[12] the Roman centurion with the servant who was sick,[13] and the Samaritan woman who had five husbands.[14]

Now stop and imagine the God who has declared Himself to be holy, righteous, loving, forgiving, and just, being unconcerned about rebellion, murder, witchcraft, abuse, perversion, injustice, unforgiveness, bullying, hatred, and stealing. You can't imagine it, can you? Nor can I.

We're not finished with this chapter yet, but it might be helpful to just *pause for a moment and reflect*: Would you really feel safe with a Father who was unmoved by these things?

Let's move on now.

What was God's passionate anger intended to achieve? First of all, it was intended to show that He is holy and will not in any way, shape, or form be in agreement with corruption. Remember Jesus in His Father's house, when He saw the moneymakers at work within it?

> In the temple courts he found men selling cattle, sheep and doves, and others sitting at tables exchanging money. So he made a whip out of cords, and drove all from the temple area, both sheep and cattle; he scattered the coins of the money-changers and overturned their tables. To those who sold doves he said, "Get these out of here! How dare you turn my Father's house into a market!"
>
> (John 2:14–16)

Sin is the relationship killer. Pure, undefiled, incorruptible God cannot and will not, to any degree, compromise with wrong; otherwise He would not be pure, undefiled, and incorruptible.[15] Does that make sense? Sin is not harmful because it is forbidden. It is forbidden because it is harmful.

Secondly, and this is so important to understand, God's passionate anger was intended to produce the result of driving His people back to Him for safety, not away from Him. They were already away from Him.

He would, after seemingly endless longsuffering, patient waiting, and warning, remove His hand – which immediately removes His hedge of protection.[16] The enemy is thus free to trample where he previously could not.[17] When life under the enemy finally took its inevitable toll, the people would turn to the Lord and cry out for His help. And always, always, the help would come in the form of a *person*.

Take time to read the events recorded in Judges chapters 2, 3, 4, 6,

10, and 13. Chapter after chapter, the pattern is repeated. The people reject God and do evil. In righteous anger the Lord steps back. The enemy comes in and oppresses them. They cry out to the Lord. He raises up a deliverer. They come back to the God who loves them. Throughout these chapters one deliverer after another comes on the scene: Othniel, Ehud, Deborah, Gideon, Jephthah, and finally Samson.

Everything God says and does is underpinned by a depth of love we can barely comprehend.[18] If it has to be tough love, it will be tough love.

The cold truth is that where there is no reverential fear of God, we drift away slowly but surely into the world's godless ways, and we gradually, layer by layer, come under the influence of the god of this world. Jesus told His listeners never to fear other people but always to maintain a healthy, reverential fear for His Father. In the next breath He was telling them that they were so individually precious to God that even the very hairs upon their heads were numbered by the One who loves them. Do you see the healthy balance? In reverentially fearing God, you have no need to fear anybody or anything else.

> Do not be afraid of those who kill the body but cannot kill the soul. Rather, be afraid of the One who can destroy both soul and body in hell. Are not two sparrows sold for a penny? Yet not one of them will fall to the ground apart from the will of your Father. And even the very hairs of your head are all numbered. So don't be afraid; you are worth more than many sparrows.
>
> (Matthew 10:28–31)

The more we fix our eyes on the world, the more we become enticed into becoming friends with the world and its ways.

Ponder this verse and the sensitive, passionate heart behind it:

> You adulterous people, don't you know that friendship with the world is hatred towards God? Anyone who chooses to be a friend of

the world becomes an enemy of God. Or do you think Scripture says without reason that the spirit he caused to live in us envies intensely?

(James 4:4–5)

It is truly amazing that God is actually jealous for a real relationship with you and me. He wants Him and us – not Him and us and the god of this world subtly woven into the relationship. He will not play "second fiddle." He wants us to be hot or cold – not lukewarm.[19] Listen, He desires *all* our love, not some of our love.

God the Father spoke this through Moses to the children of Israel:

Love the LORD your God with all your heart and with all your soul and with all your strength.

(Deuteronomy 6:5)

And He repeats it to us through His Son Jesus.[20] His desire for *your* heart has not weakened. He does not want a half-hearted relationship with you.

How does it make you feel when you realize that God, *your* Heavenly Father, is passionate for *your* love? That He puts a great value on *your* love for Him? That His Spirit within you "yearns jealously"[21] for *you*?

He hates it when you love the world and its ways instead of Him and His ways – or when you mix the two together as of equal value. Jesus says, "Follow Me," and the god of this world also says, "Follow me." We must choose whom we will serve, because there is no middle ground.

I could not worship, nor feel safe with, a wishy-washy, passive Creator who cared little for what I was doing with my life. Never despise the righteous anger of God. It means that He is a Father who is rightfully angry at the things that destroy us. Rather, honor and cherish this aspect of our Father who is in heaven.[22] In truth it is our safeguard. We default to foolish. We default to carnal. We default to lukewarm.

The healthy, reverential fear of the Lord is the beginning of wisdom.[23]

Where to now?

God the Father raised up deliverers again and again, but they were only temporary deliverers. One day He would send The Deliverer. The Permanent Deliverer.

And that's where we are going next . . .

Notes

1. Leviticus 20:1–3.
2. Exodus 22:22–24.
3. Exodus 22:25–27.
4. Exodus 22:21.
5. Leviticus 18; 20.
6. Proverbs 9:10.
7. John 10:37.
8. Luke 7:22.
9. Mark 1:34.
10. Luke 19:1–9.
11. Luke 8:43–44.
12. Matthew 15:21–28.
13. Matthew 8:5–11.
14. John 4:4–26.
15. Isaiah 1:4.
16. Job 1:10.
17. Isaiah 5:5.
18. 1 John 4:8.
19. Revelation 3:16.
20. Matthew 22:37.
21. James 4:5 NKJV.
22. Hebrews 12:5.
23. Psalm 111:10.

CHAPTER 7

THE SUFFERING
FATHER

It is a cold, wet January morning as I write this, and I am wondering how to deal with this central chapter. It should be the most powerful chapter of all.

Here's what I am thinking. I have a wonderful family. We are very close-knit. I like to think that if it came to the bit, I would be willing to die in order to save one or more of them.

I have a wonderful, faithful, sacrificial ministry team, some of whom have been with me on this remarkable journey for more than twelve years. I truly honor and treasure them all, from the depth of my being. Trust me, they are good people. Would I be willing to die in order to save one or more of them? I will continue to do my best to live for them, but if I'm honest, I'm not sure if I could actually *die* for them. Especially if it involved great suffering.

However, I have no need to ponder the following: Under no circumstances could I let one of my children die to save anyone – family, friends, or team. I believe – no, I am certain – that I would find it relatively easy to throw myself in front of an oncoming car in order to save my wife or one of my children, but I could not let my wife or one of my children throw themselves in front of an oncoming car to save me or anyone else.

So while, under the right circumstances, I like to think that I would be willing to die for someone I love deeply – a good person – under no circumstances could I cope with the thought of one of my sons or my daughter doing the same. I am not the first person to agonize over this train of thought and to ask, "What if?" The Apostle Paul wrote this:

> Very rarely will anyone die for a righteous man, though for a good man someone might possibly dare to die.
>
> (Romans 5:7)

So if I saw you needed to be saved, and I stepped forward to die in your place in order that you might live, then you would know beyond doubt that to me your life was of immense worth.

Now, step into the realms beyond that if you can. I struggle to, but see if you can.

If you needed to be saved, and I sent my son to die in your place in order that you might live, then forever, and ever, through happy days and through sad days, through riches or through poverty, through sickness or through health, you would know beyond doubt that to me, your life was of unimaginable worth. There would be no greater thing that I could do. Nothing would cost me as much as that. My son would suffer for you, but I would suffer more as I watched.

Father God could have sent Michael the archangel to take on human flesh and die for us (as Jehovah's Witnesses teach), but in our hearts we would know that that would have cost God the Father little. He could create more angels.

A begotten son is different.

King David's son Absalom rebelled against him and conspired to take the throne for himself. He caused his father a lot of pain. David was, in truth, a pretty poor example of a father, and Absalom was a pretty poor example of a son. And yet . . . And yet when Absalom was killed after a battle, we hear his father's real pain – and the declaration that he would rather have died than his son.

> The king was shaken. He went up to the room over the gateway and wept. As he went, he said: "O my son Absalom! My son, my son Absalom! If only I had died instead of you – O Absalom, my son, my son!"
>
> (2 Samuel 18:33)

I state again that the hardest thing in the world is for a father to see his son (or daughter) going through pain or encountering death. Ask any parent what their greatest fear is.

Remember Abraham? How much he longed for a son through his wife Sarah, a son that would be flesh of his flesh, bone of his bone. And God promised him that one day he would have that longed-for son through Sarah. After a long delay, Isaac was born: the son of promise. Can you or I begin to imagine how precious he was to Abraham?

Then one day God the Father did a strange thing. On the surface it seemed like a very cruel thing. He asked Abraham to put his only begotten son on an altar and sacrifice him. If God had asked Abraham to lay himself on the altar and let Isaac kill him, it would have been easier. But that's not what God asked of him.

As father and son made their way up the mountainside to make a "sacrifice," Isaac innocently asked, "Where is the lamb?"[1]

Abraham replied, not fully understanding that he was speaking out one of the most powerful prophecies ever recorded in Scripture, "God himself will provide the lamb . . ."[2]

When the altar was prepared with stones, and the wood placed upon the stones, Abraham bound his son with cords and laid him upon that crude altar. Can you imagine Abraham's pain at this point? Deep down, he would have been clinging to a seed of hope. The writer of the book of Hebrews says that he was trusting that God would somehow bring Isaac back to life again, since God had promised that all nations would be blessed through him, and if Isaac was not brought back to life then that promise could not be fulfilled.[3]

Yet can you imagine the pain of the father as he raised the knife to slay his only son? Did they make eye contact? Was Abraham weeping or was he silent with trauma? Did he waver and lower the knife once or twice, before finally setting his chin like flint to obey? We can only imagine.

Suddenly – and I love God's "suddenly" even though it always seems to come at the last minute of the darkest hour – the angel of the Lord called out to him saying, "Do not lay a hand on the boy."[4] And there nearby, trapped in a bush by its horns, was a ram that could be used on the altar.

Can you imagine the relief of the father as he took his son, unscathed, off that crude altar and hugged him? I'm sure he must have sat down and wept with relief that he did not have to see his son slain before his very eyes.

Two thousand years later the exercise was to be repeated – on the exact same mountain. A Father permitted His only Son, whom He loved,[5] to be bound to a crude wooden altar after receiving a terrible beating. This time there was to be no last-minute reprieve. No ram to replace the Son. The Son was the Ram, once and for all time replacing the millions of rams that had been sacrificed for the people's sins. The greatest act of sacrificial love the world has ever seen: a Father lets His beloved Son be tortured, humiliated, spat upon, and crucified.

So that . . .

So that . . .

So that you, and I, could be saved, and be able to come home to Him.

This is rightly the most famous verse in the Bible. Feel God's heart in this:

> For God so loved the world that he gave his one and only Son, that whoever believes in him shall not perish but have eternal life. For

God did not send his Son into the world to condemn the world, but to save the world through him.

(John 3:16–17)

Saved? What does that mean? It means that a way was made, a door opened, a chasm bridged, so that you, precious one, could come home to *your* Heavenly Father. So that *your* name could be written into the family Book of Life.[6] So that *you* could move from a position of eternal separation from God to eternal life with God.

Here's the truth and we need to own it: Adam sinned and separated himself from his Creator. All his descendants, to this day, carry that sinful disposition.[7] He was a sinner. My lovely father and mother were sinners. I am a sinner.[8] My children are sinners. You are a sinner.[9] Your lovely children will be sinners.

Your sins and mine are foul. Rotten. Stinking. The little ones and the big ones. Never try to spray them with the excuse of good intentions to try and make them smell sweet.

The wages of sin are death.[10] There is no natural escape from that.

In the Gulf War in 1991, the world saw for the first time the ability of American missiles to hit a target with pinpoint accuracy. Once a laser locked on to the target, the death-bringing missile would land there in due time. There was no escape. No hiding place.

We are eternal beings. Or to be more accurate, we are a trinity made up of spirit, soul, and body,[11] and while our spirit and soul are eternal, our body is merely a tent that is perishing and returning to the dust from whence it came.[12]

Eternal death does not mean the extinguishing of our whole being. A total ending. A nothing. While this earthly body gradually deteriorates and is then gone forever, we, as spiritual beings with a soul, live on for eternity. Hang in here now – this is important. Eternity is a long time to spend in the wrong place.

There's heaven, which is much advertised, and there's hell, which is rarely talked about. But it is real, and Jesus spoke of it several times, and He does not tell lies.[13]

Hell is a place designed for the devil. That's where he and his angels are going,[14] and those who are his.[15]

I heard it put this way and it made it easy to understand: Wherever the train driver goes is where his passengers are going. The devil's train is hell-bound,[16] while Jesus' passengers are heaven-bound.[17] Are you still submitted to and following the invisible but very real god of this world, or are you submitted to and following Jesus?[18] Choose which train you will get on and stay on.

When Jesus says "Follow Me," it means that where He goes, we go.

> Do not let your hearts be troubled. Trust in God; trust also in me. In my Father's house are many rooms; if it were not so, I would have told you. I am going there to prepare a place for you. And if I go and prepare a place for you, I will come back and take you to be with me that you also may be where I am.
>
> (John 14:1–3)

God the Father does not want anyone to be lost.[19] But He gives us that frightening thing called free will.[20]

There is nothing defiling coming into heaven.[21] Otherwise it would cease to be heaven. If it helps, imagine a white carpet in your home, and people at the front door with muddy boots. You and I are not getting into heaven dressed in our own righteousness.[22] Our muddy boots. Our defilement through sin.

Ever told a wee white lie? Sorry to be so blunt, but there's no other way to put it: You're a liar. Ever taken a paper clip or a pen from work that was not yours to take? You're a thief. You and I both need a deliverer: a heaven-sent Savior. We need someone completely without sin of His own[23] who is willing to be punished for our sins. (If He had His own sin, He would be getting punished for His own sin, not mine and yours.)

God the Father sent that Person. That once-for-all-time Deliverer.[24]

His only begotten Son. This was the Father's greatest act of love for a fallen world.

> This is how God showed his love among us: He sent his one and only Son into the world that we might live through him.
>
> (1 John 4:9)

"That *we* might live through Him." We must humbly acknowledge that we cannot be saved through our own good behavior.[25] Even if you are a good person who has lived a good life, you still have sin in your life.

The events at the cross, the establishment of the New Covenant between God and humankind, is sometimes rightly called the "Divine Exchange." Maybe this illustration of mine will make it crystal clear:

The Divine Exchange of the New Covenant

For God took the sinless Christ and poured into him our sins.
Then, in exchange, he poured God's goodness into us!
(2 Corinthians 5:21 LB)

He was chastised that we might have peace . . .
God laid on him the guilt and sins of every one of us.
(Isaiah 53:5a, 6 LB)

I remember flying into Dallas, Texas, shortly after the terrible events of 9/11 in New York. You can imagine what the security was like (and still is). My hand luggage was screened and cleared, but then to my surprise I "beeped" as I passed through the electronic doorway. Immediately, I was called over for a more detailed search. The guard did his job well and asked me to pass through the screening doorway once more, but still I "beeped." He checked my shoes, pockets, and under my collar. But still I "beeped." I was not getting into the USA until I was declared clean!

Eventually we found the offending matter. A minute, really minute, piece of aluminum foil from a packet of headache tablets was lying in the bottom of the breast pocket of my shirt. I could hardly believe that something so small could bar me from entry into the richest country in the world. After all, I was a good person.

Good person, if you have, or have had, even one tiny sin in your life, you will not gain entry into God's House – into heaven. If God were to let you in with your minute sin, then He would have to allow in the next person with just a little bit more. And so on. No sin will enter heaven. It is clean and undefiled, and will forever stay that way.

If we do not accept God's one and only solution, then we stay, forever, outside heaven. We must acknowledge that we need a Savior to take upon Himself the judgment and the punishment that is rightly ours.[26] There is no room for pride here at all. We must acknowledge that we are truly intent on laying down our rebellion (being the boss of our own lives) and acknowledge the resurrected Jesus as the Lord of our lives. That's it. Simple, available, and instant.

> . . . if you confess with your mouth, "Jesus is Lord," and believe in your heart that God raised him from the dead, you will be saved.
>
> (Romans 10:9)

Is this exclusive? Yes, because there is only one way to God: through Jesus, His Son.[27] Yet it is also totally inclusive, because "every tribe and language and people and nation" may come.[28]

Here's a good prayer if you are not already saved. It is not a formula, but simply some words that might sum up that deep desire within you to be "right with God" and to walk with God.

Lord Jesus, I acknowledge that I am a sinner. I acknowledge that I have sinned against You in word, thought, and deed.

But now, Lord Jesus, I turn away from ALL my sin and my rebellion, and I turn to You alone as my Lord and my Savior.

I believe that You shed Your precious blood and died on the cross for me – and that You rose again from the dead – in order that I might be able to come home to Your Father, and now my Father, as a newborn child of God.

I thankfully receive my complete forgiveness through Your finished work on the cross, and I ask You to fill me with the Holy Spirit. From this moment on, I boast only of You as my Lord and my God!

And then (I love this part) there is great rejoicing in heaven![29]

Time to stop and reflect. The following few questions just need a simple "Yes" or "No."

Does God compromise with sin?

Are you a sinner?

Was the slow painful death of Jesus a selfish or a selfless act?

Did it come from a heart of love, or a heart of anger?

Does the sacrificial death of God's Son on the cross for you give you a) some value? b) quite a lot of value? c) immense value?

Notes

1. Genesis 22:7.
2. Genesis 22:8.
3. Hebrews 11:17–19.
4. Genesis 22:12.
5. Matthew 3:17.
6. Revelation 21:27.
7. Romans 5:12.
8. Psalm 51:5.
9. Romans 3:23.
10. Romans 6:23.
11. 1 Thessalonians 5:23.
12. 2 Corinthians 5:1.
13. Matthew 5:29.
14. Revelation 20:10.
15. Revelation 20:15.
16. Revelation 20:10.
17. John 14:1–3.
18. 1 John 5:19.
19. 2 Peter 3:9.
20. Revelation 3:20.
21. Revelation 21:27.
22. Romans 10:3.
23. Hebrews 4:15.
24. Hebrews 7:27; 9:26.
25. Philippians 3:9.
26. Colossians 1:19–21.
27. John 14:6.
28. Revelation 5:9.
29. Luke 15:4–6.

CHAPTER 8

DOES GOD REALLY WANT TO BE A FATHER TO *YOU*?

There are two ways to have a child. One is where you have a child "naturally" (you know what I mean). The other way is to adopt.

The first way, you get what you get – you have no choice in the matter. The child could be a boy or a girl, an introvert or an extrovert, and so on. Adoption is different: You get to see what you could have. You get the full history of the child: the good, the bad, and the ugly. There are no surprises.

God the Father knows who you are. He knows your full history: the good, the bad, and yes, the ugly. (You may blush here!) Nothing hidden. No surprises.

Except one. The surprise is that knowing you, and knowing me, He deeply desires you and me to be His child. That we would call Him "Abba" Father.

Listen to what Paul wrote:

> For you did not receive the spirit of bondage again to fear, but you received the *Spirit of adoption* by whom we cry out, "Abba, Father."
> (Romans 8:15 NKJV, emphasis mine)

Listen to what Jesus said:

> But as many as received Him, to them He gave the right to *become children of God*, to those who believe in His name.
>
>   (John 1:12 NKJV, emphasis mine)

God not only wants you in His family forever – He has also actively pursued you. He leads your steps to Jesus. Listen again to what Jesus said:

> No one can come to Me unless the Father who sent Me draws him . . .
>   (John 6:44a NKJV)

So there you have it. Lord God Almighty, Creator of heaven and earth, Omnipotent One, Omnipresent One, deeply desires that He and you would have a Father and child relationship. He knew, and still knows, all about you. Everything. The lot. He sent Jesus to make the one and only way for you to be able to come to Him. He drew you to Jesus. He adopted you. You are of unimaginable value to Him.

In a world where rejection is commonplace, that is hard to grasp, isn't it? But it's true. And if you are struggling to take *that* truth on board, there's more.

To help you grasp this "more," I need to tell you a story – actually, several stories. They helped me to understand, so I trust they will help you.

My father died nearly two decades ago. My mother sold up all that they owned in their rented house, raising just enough capital to buy a small semi-detached bungalow where she saw out the remainder of her days. When she died, she left a simple will. Her only possession, the little pensioner bungalow, was to be sold and the money divided equally between her three children. After expenses, there was £24,000 left.

The solicitor handling the will called me and my two sisters to her office and invited us to sit down in front of her desk.

"Well," she said, "you are all joint heirs."

In other words, what I got as the firstborn son, my sister Shireen got. And what Shireen got, my sister Jill got. And what Jill got, I got. In other words, Mum had made no difference whatsoever between us.

Then I remembered a verse of Scripture that I had never taken note of before. And when I turned it up again in the book of Romans I was shocked. It was the follow-on from Paul telling us that as adopted children we could call God our Father "Abba." Here's what Paul wrote in full:

> For you did not receive the spirit of bondage again to fear, but you received the Spirit of adoption by whom we cry out, "Abba, Father." The Spirit Himself bears witness with our spirit that we are children of God, and if children, then heirs – heirs of God and *joint heirs with Christ*, if indeed we suffer with Him, that we may also be glorified together.
>
> (Romans 8:15–17 NKJV, emphasis mine)

In the book of Galatians (in which Paul was writing to the church members in Galatia) he described us as heirs with Christ,[1] but in the passage above, writing to the early church members in Rome, he expands on that and calls us "joint heirs" with Jesus. Joint heirs – with Jesus the Christ, the Messiah?

Yes. You are called into the family of God to be a joint heir with Jesus. How's that for a destiny? This means that God makes no difference between adopted *you* and His only begotten Son. No difference.

Let me give you an example of God's heart for you on this matter. Where is Jesus seated right now? He is seated, enthroned, at the right hand of the Father. At the right hand of our Father, *who is in heaven*.

The Apostle Paul wrote to the church at Ephesus:

> . . . He raised Him [Jesus] from the dead and seated Him at His right hand in the heavenly places, far above all principality and power and

might and dominion, and every name that is named, not only in this
age but also in that which is to come. And He put all things under
His feet, and gave Him to be head over all things to the church.

(Ephesians 1:20–22 NKJV)

No theological surprises there. We understand that. But here's the
surprise: You might be firmly nailed to this planet for three score years
and ten, or whatever; but in *position*, God the Father has placed
you "legally" next to Him, "seated" in heavenly places, because you are
"in Christ."

Paul, just four verses later, unpacked this to the church:

But because of his *great love* for us, God, who is rich in mercy, made
us alive with Christ even when we were dead in transgressions – it is
by grace you have been saved. And God raised us up with Christ and
seated us with him in the heavenly realms in Christ Jesus.

(Ephesians 2:4–6, emphasis mine)

You in Christ, and Christ in you. Inseparable.[2] One in spirit, joined
with the Lord.[3] How does this work? You and I are here on earth, while
Christ is in heaven, seated at the Father's right hand. Well, He is the
head and we are the body. Wherever the head is, so is the body.

Pastor Carter Conlon of Times Square Church, New York, puts it
this way: When an athlete is sprinting for the finishing line, he leans
forward so that his head breaks through the finishing tape first. At that
moment, often caught in slow motion or on still camera, the head has
finished the race while the body is still on the track but following the
head across the finish line.

Where He is, there you shall be also.[4] Could God draw you any
closer to Himself? Right next to Himself "in Christ."

God the Father called His only begotten Son "beloved." What a
tender word to use!

And suddenly a voice came from heaven, saying, "This is My beloved Son, in whom I am well pleased."

(Matthew 3:17 NKJV)

If He calls Jesus beloved, it follows that if you are a joint heir with Jesus, He would tenderly call you beloved as well. Does He? Yes, indeed He does! Again and again and again, God's Spirit caused the apostles to speak that tender word of love to His children. Below are a few examples from the more than fifty times the word "beloved" is used of believers, individually or corporately as the Body of Christ (all emphasis mine).

(Try saying "beloved" fifty times to get the point God is making!)

To all who are in Rome, *beloved* of God, called to be saints . . .

(Romans 1:7 NKJV)

Beloved, do not avenge yourselves . . .

(Romans 12:19 NKJV)

Therefore, having these promises, *beloved* . . .

(2 Corinthians 7:1 NKJV)

But we are bound to give thanks to God always for you . . . *beloved* by the Lord . . .

(2 Thessalonians 2:13 NKJV)

But you, *beloved*, building yourselves up on your most holy faith . . .

(Jude 1:20 NKJV)

Singapore teacher Joseph Prince rightly points out that when the devil was tempting Jesus in the wilderness, he carefully, deliberately, omitted one word of what the Father had said about Jesus at the River Jordan just days earlier. Remember what the Father had said about Jesus?

This is My beloved Son, in whom I am well pleased.

(Matthew 3:17 NKJV)

But Satan did not say to Jesus, "If you are the beloved Son of God . . ." Instead he said, "If you are the Son of God . . ."[5] This is a *big* difference. When Satan comes against you, he will always omit the word "beloved." If he reminded you of your place in your Father's heart, his power to heap condemnation on you for your failures would be broken. Remember that. And remember this: Beloved, you really are be-loved. So be loved!

Here's the next story.

A well-known evangelist, now deceased, had one "natural" teenage boy. He and his wife decided to adopt another teenage boy. (How brave is that?) They assured this nervous young man that he was now and forever a full member of the family. There was no difference between him and the natural son. No difference. But no matter how well and how often this was explained to him, it was obvious that this truth was only head-knowledge to the young man, rather than a heart-truth. I am sure we could all identify with the young man. It is a lot to take in.

Teenagers eat a lot. And in the middle of the night the parents would hear a bedroom door open and footsteps heading downstairs and into the kitchen. Then they would hear cornflakes being poured into a bowl, the fridge opening and closing as milk was lifted out and poured over the cereal. Soon they would hear the bowl being thrown into the sink, along with the spoon, for Mum to wash up in the morning. Then the footsteps heading back upstairs, and finally the bedroom door being closed. Then silence.

Until perhaps thirty minutes later. Then they would hear another bedroom door opening quietly. Footsteps creeping down the stairs, stopping for a moment every time one of the stairs creaked loudly. They heard the kitchen door opening quietly; they knew the fridge door was being opened but they couldn't hear that. They could just make out the sound of a bowl being lifted down from a cupboard shelf; just make out the sound of cornflakes being gently slidden from their box into the bowl. They could hear the sound of the bowl and spoon being washed, and moments later, being set carefully back onto the cupboard shelf. Finally, they could hear the gentle, careful steps, heading back up to the bedroom, and the door being closed ever so slowly.

The parents said it broke their hearts.

But . . .

But one night they heard two bedroom doors opening, two sets of footsteps clattering down the stairs, two bowls, two cornflake feeds, and two bowls and two spoons being thrown into the sink for Mum to wash up in the morning. Finally two sets of noisy footsteps returning to two bedrooms. And the parents cried with joy. At last the young man understood.

Your Heavenly Father has declared that you and Jesus are joint heirs. We acknowledge this immense statement with a polite nod of our heads. Can you imagine how your Heavenly Father longs for you to grasp His heart's intent for you?

Let's look at this strange word "Abba" for a moment. It is not an English word, but originally an Aramaic word which became part of the Hebrew language. I can think of no easier way to explain it than this: Go to any city in the West and people-watch for a while. Imagine for a moment a father and child walking past, hand in hand. The child wants an ice cream. "Daddy," the child says, "can I have an ice cream?"

Now imagine doing the same in present-day Jerusalem. Only this time, you hear the child saying, "Abba, can I have an ice cream?" "Abba" is just a personal term for a father – "Daddy."

If a stranger came to my house and one of my children opened the door, the stranger might say, "Can I speak to your father, please?" My child would turn and shout back into the home saying, "Daddy, there's someone here to see you." The stranger calls me "father;" my child calls me "Daddy."

In the time of the Old Testament the Israelites knew God as Yahweh. In fact so "distant" did God seem to them that they would use only the letters YHWH. Imagine the shock, then, when the disciples first heard Jesus talk to YHWH and refer to Him as "*Abba*, Father."[6]

As joint heirs, let's look at our written invitation to call God the Father "Abba" as Jesus did.

> For you did not receive the spirit of bondage again to fear, but you received the Spirit of adoption by whom *we cry out*, "Abba, Father."
>
> (Romans 8:15 NKJV, emphasis mine)

> And because you are sons, God has sent forth the Spirit of His Son into *your hearts, crying out*, "Abba, Father!"
>
> (Galatians 4:6 NKJV, emphasis mine)

I used to think that there were some passages in the Bible that God did not come out too well in. I would never have said that out loud, but sometimes I thought it. Below is one example. Jesus told this story and He was clearly speaking about His Father.

(Bible publishers usually place a descriptive title above this story such as "A friend calls at midnight.")

> And He said to them, "Which of you shall have a friend, and go to him at midnight and say to him, 'Friend, lend me three loaves; for a friend of mine has come to me on his journey, and I have nothing to set before him;' and he will answer from within and say, 'Do not trouble me; the door is now shut, and my children are with me in bed; I cannot rise and give to you'? I say to you, though he will not rise and give to him because he is his friend, yet because of his persistence he will rise and give him as many as he needs."
>
> (Luke 11:5–8 NKJV)

Jesus immediately went on to say,

> So I say to you, ask, and it will be given to you; seek, and you will find; knock, and it will be opened to you. For everyone who asks receives, and he who seeks finds, and to him who knocks it will be opened.
>
> (Luke 11:9–10 NKJV)

I could understand this call to be persistent in prayer, and that is certainly one of several lessons that Jesus was giving to His listeners. But I confess that I did not like the idea of being locked outside the Father's house, and only being able to get His brief attention when I persisted in banging on His door.

Then I read what Ken Gire wrote about this story in his book *Moments with the Savior: A Devotional Life of Christ*, and I saw it! Oh, how I saw it! It was *a friend* knocking at the door. Where were the children? They were inside the house, safely tucked up in bed with their Father! In the story that Jesus told, the Father answered the friend's persistent knock but then hurried back to His children inside. That was a different viewpoint altogether.

In the ancient Middle East the houses were easy to break into. Remember the crippled man's friends breaking open the roof to lower their friend down on ropes so that he would be in front of Jesus?[7] There was no phone system to call the police if your home was broken into. The only safe place at night was being safely tucked up in bed with your big strong daddy there to protect you. Remember the reason why the Father was so hesitant to come down? "Do not trouble me; the door is now shut, and my children are with me in bed; I cannot rise and give to you."

Here is another story about how I was helped to digest this truth.

As a young man trying to make his way through life, I was given the opportunity to join a leading advertising agency as an "account executive." One of my first jobs was to handle the recruitment advertising for an international company that manufactured man-made fibers. It was a huge company with a workforce of 850. The workers were divided into eight-hour shift workers and twelve-hour shift workers.

This was in the era when there were more jobs than workers, and workers were so hard to get and to keep that advertisers had to be very bold and persistent in their advertising if they wanted to ensure a full workforce.

On my first visit to meet the personnel officer, he explained to me that the previous half-page advertisements for twelve-hour shift workers had been so successful that they now had many more men than they needed, but that no one seemed to want the eight-hour shift job. (This was because although the twelve-hour work shifts were 50% longer, the pay was 50% more!) As the company now desperately needed eight-hour shift workers, he asked me to place their previously used half-page advertisement for eight-hour shift workers into every newspaper in Northern Ireland. Yes, into every newspaper. As an advertising agency, we got commission of 15% on all advertising placed through us, so this was a very good morning's work so early in my career.

I duly went back to the office, looked up the scrapbook where this client's previous advertisements were pasted (this was pre-computers), and noted the dates and newspapers that they had previously appeared in. So it was just a matter of writing out an order form to every newspaper in the country, telling them to repeat the half-page advertisement for this client that had appeared previously on such and such a date. What could be simpler?

Come the Wednesday when the first of the newspapers was published, I noticed that the first paper I checked had mistakenly placed the wrong half-page advertisement. They had placed the twelve-hour shift advertisement instead of the eight-hour. Too bad, I thought, they will have to replace it with the correct one in the next edition at their own expense.

Then I opened the next paper and it had the twelve-hour shift advertisement. And the next paper. And the next paper.

In a state of near-terror I ran down to the admin office, opened the client's scrapbook, and saw that the relevant dates were written *above* the newspaper cuttings, not below them as I had thought. I had, at the beginning of my career with this leading agency, placed the wrong half-page advertisement into every newspaper in the country. My new boss was going to have to pay for the wrong ones, and I would almost certainly lose my job.

I shared the office with another young executive, and I quietly asked him to leave me alone for a while. I went into a corner of the office and got down on my knees, and I beat on heaven's door.

"Help me, God!" I cried. "I need a miracle, and I need your mercy. Help me, God."

Suddenly, after half an hour of beating on heaven's door, I was overcome by a strange peace. My fear had gone. I went to my desk and phoned the personnel officer.

"I've made a terrible mistake," I said. "I've mistakenly placed the wrong advertisement into every newspaper in the country."

I waited for the inevitable reply, which would be along the lines that as it was our company's fault, it was up to us to put the correct advertisement in the papers next week at our own expense. But after a moment's silence that's not what he said.

"Put the eight-hour shift in next week and we will pay for both weeks. We'll just add the replies we got this week on to the waiting list for twelve-hour shifts."

Was I hearing him right? Not only were we not going to have to pay for our (my) mistake, but also we were now getting an extra week of half-page advertising in every newspaper in Northern Ireland as a result of my mistake?

That was indeed what happened. As I reflected on this incident many years later, and now as a Christian, I realized that I was that friend of God who beat upon His door, and eventually I got my "three loaves."

I say I was a friend of God and indeed I was. I had always believed in God and in Jesus Christ, His only begotten Son. As I said at the beginning of this book, I had said prayers every night of my life since I was three years of age. Sometimes I would pray for up to an hour on my knees at night. I attended church every Sunday. I took Communion; I hosted a cell group in my house every fortnight. But Jesus was not my Lord. I was the master, or the Lord, of my life. There were a few secret sins that I had no intention at that stage of turning away from, so the best term I could use to describe myself then was "a friend of God."

But now I am His child. His son. And I am safely inside my Father's house. I only have to whisper "Abba" and I know I have His ear. Here is the mystery now revealed: The Door to the Father's House is a Person – Jesus.

> I am the door. If anyone enters by Me, he will be saved, and will go in and out and find pasture.
>
> (John 10:9 NKJV)

And on 11 August 1989 I entered my Father's House through that Door. There are many times I feel the need to persist in prayer over one situation or another, but never do I feel like the "friend" locked outside anymore. I'm in my Dad's House, and I'm safe. So are you.

Time to stop and reflect.

Are you, *even you*, truly wanted by God?

Did you have to chase after God or did He come looking for you?

Will you be viewed as a second-rate child in His family, or a full family member with all the rights and privileges of a true family member?

Have you grasped the truth that Lord God Almighty invites you, His child, to join Jesus in calling Him "Daddy" or "Dad"?

Have you understood what the term "joint heir" means?

As a child of God, are you inside the House or outside?

Are *you* beloved? Really, really His beloved?

Will you let yourself be loved by God?

Notes

1. Galatians 4:7.
2. Romans 8:35.
3. 1 Corinthians 6:17.
4. John 14:3.

5. Luke 4:3.
6. Mark 14:36.
7. Mark 2:4.

CHAPTER 9

HINDRANCES TO RECEIVING THE FATHER'S HEART

As people, we all have three basic needs in life: to belong, to be valued, and to be loved. If one or more of these needs is missing, we can become emotionally damaged. When someone is emotionally damaged they become vulnerable. Thus the "god of this world" will, throughout your life, attempt to make you believe that you don't belong, that your life is of no value, and that no one really loves you. The measure to which the devil succeeds in doing this is the measure to which you will be unable to receive your Heavenly Father's love.

In this chapter we are going to look at some of the hindrances that might stop *you* understanding, receiving, and responding to the true heart of God. Let's think about some of the words that people often use to describe their father.

DISMISSIVE

Was your father generally dismissive towards you? Perhaps as a child you wanted to tell him about the fun you had, or the fall you had, but he was always "too busy right now" to listen. Maybe it made you feel worthless. After all, if you were worth listening to, wouldn't he have listened? It must have been something wrong with you. So guess what? You think your Heavenly Father is "too busy right now" to listen to you.

The truth, though, is different from "the truth of your experience."

> Then you will call upon me and come and pray to me, *and I will listen to you.*
>
> (Jeremiah 29:12, emphasis mine)

DISTANT

Was your father always in the background of your life rather than in the foreground? You shared the same house, but, like ships passing in the night, you rarely saw much of him. Perhaps you saw him invest his time in other people and in other pursuits, but rarely investing his time in you. Naturally you might conclude, "It's my fault. I am insignificant. If I was significant to my father, he would invest some of his time in me." So in your experience the truth is that "fathers are always distant figures."

Therefore God the Father might be a distant figure to you. After all, He dwells in "the heavens," even in the "third heaven," so of course He would be a distant figure. You cannot imagine God the Father drawing close to you, because you see yourself as insignificant.

The truth is somewhat different. Your Heavenly Father loves it when you want to draw close to Him. Your heart's desire is significant to Him.

> But when you pray, go into your room, close the door and pray to *your* Father, who is unseen. Then *your* Father, who sees what is done in secret, will reward you.
>
> (Matthew 6:6, emphasis mine)

SILENT

Maybe your father did not communicate with you, in that he never said much to you about his thoughts or feelings, or even what his plans were for the future. In fact, if he never said much about *anything*, then the result will be that as a child, you think that you are the problem. You believe that the reason your father won't communicate with you is because you do not matter to him. You eventually come to believe that you are just not worth the effort to speak to.

So when you attempt to approach Father God, you just assume that Father God doesn't want to speak to you either – that to God, you just really aren't worth the effort. In fact, you don't expect to hear anything from God so you don't ever "waste your time" trying to listen to Him speak to you. As a result, you never do hear God speak to you, Spirit to spirit, because you're not listening with your heart, and this only seems to confirm your belief that God does not want to speak to you.

You hear other Christians talking endlessly about their communication with God, which also fuels your belief that you are indeed the problem. God speaks. He has spoken to you already many times before now. You may not consciously remember a time when God spoke to you directly, but He has been speaking. He will illuminate certain scriptures that you just know are for you, at the point where you are right now in your life. Sometimes He'll use a book, a friend, a pastor, a movie, a song, creation . . . The list is endless really. The great writer C.S. Lewis said, "A young man who wishes to remain a sound atheist cannot be too careful of his reading."

Just because you are not hearing the heavens thunder doesn't mean God isn't speaking to you. One of the reasons that Christians today do struggle to hear God speak to them directly is because we have been taught to hate silence. We have car radios on when driving, television on at home, MP3 player on when out for a run – anything but silence. Yet the Bible tells us:

Be still, and know that I am God . . .

(Psalm 46:10)

He makes me lie down in green pastures,
   he leads me beside quiet waters,
he restores my soul.

(Psalm 23:2–3)

Learn to love silence, for in the silence God speaks into the stillness with our spirit. Spirit to spirit.[1] Deep calling to deep.[2]

Be still before the LORD and wait patiently for him . . .

(Psalm 37:7)

NON-AFFIRMING

A "non-affirming" father means a father who never complimented you in anything you did. He never said those precious, longed-for words, "Well done," and never encouraged you in anything that you attempted at home, at school, or at play. This can have a bad knock-on effect. We all need someone in authority to let us know how we are doing from time to time, and to affirm us in our efforts, and if we don't get this affirmation or guidance, then damage is likely to occur. This damage is likely to include a belief that you and all your efforts in life are unacceptable.

If your father only ever pointed out your mistakes, then your attitude towards God is likely to be that He is never happy with your efforts and focuses only on your mistakes. You could never imagine Father God saying to *you*, "Well done, good and faithful servant,"[3] or "This is My son [or daughter] in whom I am well pleased."[4] In truth, however, your real Heavenly Father is only too aware of the importance of affirmation and the damage a lack of it can do.

I can honestly say that not once, in the twenty-two years that I have been a Christian, has God said something to me that was condemning. He has gently convicted me when I've said or done something wrong, yes; challenged me, yes; condemned me, *never*.

God wants only the best for you and me. That "best" is that gradually, line by line, understanding by understanding,[5] we become more and more like Jesus.[6] How amazing!

NON-TACTILE

Yet another hindrance to receiving the heart of God is having experienced non-tactile fathering. This simply means having had a father who never made any deliberate and positive physical contact with you. Physical touch is very important – crucial, in fact. It's not surprising that the devil has targeted touch, and brought it to the point where it is almost a crime to physically touch somebody else. (Of course it should go without saying that I refer to physical touch that is non-sexual in nature and intent.)

> Greet one another with a kiss of love . . .
>
> (1 Peter 5:14)

Whenever the disciples tried ushering the children away from Jesus, He instead called them to Him, laid His hands upon them, and publicly blessed them.[7] In doing this, Jesus affirmed those kids. And remember, Jesus said, "Anyone who has seen me has seen the Father."[8]

In addition to this example, Jesus also touched the rejected "untouchable" lepers, along with many other sick and needy people. Jesus deliberately made a point of touching the untouchable. It has always been, and will always be, God's heart to affirm His children through physical touch. If God knows that we all need positive physical contact, then you can be sure that the devil will try to defile it and thus steal it from us.[9]

I remember many years ago being at a small church-meeting deep in the Irish countryside. After the meeting was over, I had gone into the church office to have a cup of tea when there was a knock on the door. Two middle-aged men came into the room with their elderly mother and asked if someone would pray for her. The elderly woman had a very large, inflamed, and swollen skin infection down the left side of her face and it was obvious that she had attempted to cover it over with lots of make-up powder. It was clear to me that the infection made the woman too embarrassed to come out during the day and that her self-consciousness over this facial issue dominated and controlled much of her life.

I took the woman's hand and listened to what Jesus would have me do. He witnessed to me that He wanted me to kiss her – right in the middle of the infection on her face. In the natural realm, this would have been impossible, but with this direction from Jesus came the ability to do it.

I said to the woman, "Jesus would like me to kiss you on the left side of your cheek – would that be OK?" The woman tearfully nodded that that would be OK, and I leaned over and kissed her right in the middle of the infection. I then said a short prayer, after which they left. I suspect that this positive physical touch meant more to that "untouchable" woman than a hundred prayers said from a distance.

If you never received physical affirmation from your father then the likely consequence is that you believe that you are somehow "unclean." This is not a conscious thought but rather a general feeling of uncleanness. To you, fathers don't come close to you, so why would Father God come close to you? Can you see that?

ABUSIVE

Abusive fathering, whether it is physical, sexual, verbal, emotional, financial, or spiritual, is *very* destructive when it comes to relating to Father God. Many Christians who were abused – and have not had good ministry into that abuse – go through life feeling no assurance that they are truly saved.

"Abuse" usually means that someone who has authority over you has used that authority for his or her selfish gain. Instead of being protected by them, you needed protection from them. "Ab-use" literally means "abnormal use." Where there has been abusive fathering, the consequential belief is: "I cannot trust anyone in authority." To you, where there is authority there is also the potential for pain. So when it comes to the ultimate Authority in life – God – then you instinctively put up defenses to protect yourself.

The fruit of this belief system, this defense system, is that you find yourself making endless excuses not to attend church, or else you go from church to church, pastor to pastor, and ministry to ministry. Anytime someone in authority gets too close to you, the alarm bells in your emotions start to ring and you make yet another excuse for leaving. To you, people in authority cannot be trusted.

If this was your experience of fatherhood, then being asked to trust Father God can be very difficult. (Remember the poem at the beginning of this book!) I encourage you to begin letting down your guard to God. Perhaps when things went wrong in the past, you blamed God, reasoning that He could and should have stopped it. If that is the case, please talk to a mature Christian about it, but better still, or in addition, please talk to God about it. Be honest with God. Don't tell Him what you think He wants to hear. Tell Him how you feel, how you fear. Tell Him you hurt. King David did this – it is recorded again and again in the Psalms – and despite his terrible mistakes he is recorded as being a "man after God's own heart."[10]

We live in a fallen world and are surrounded by fallen creatures making lots of wrong choices, some of which have severely affected us, but God came to give life – and life in abundance. The devil is the one determined to kill, steal, and destroy.[11] Be mad at the devil, not at God. The Son of God was manifested in the flesh so that the works of the devil would be destroyed.[12]

ARGUMENTATIVE

If you had an argumentative father, someone who seemed to be in conflict with everything and everybody in life, then your experience will have made you vulnerable to the belief that conflict is inevitable, simply the way of the world. In all your relationships, conflict is an everyday experience.

The outworking of this mindset is that you expect that there will always be conflict between you and God the Father. The "God of peace"[13] is only dry theology to you. Conflict communication is normal to you. If you want something, you shout. If you want to change somebody's mind about something, then you shout at them. If you want to control somebody or a situation, you shout at them. To you, everything in life has to be won by argument or else you won't get anything done in life.

Stop and think a moment about yourself and some of the people you know. Think how often conversations escalate into arguments needlessly. Think of your marriage. Are you merely repeating how you saw your parents deal with conflict? I'm certainly not saying that Christians should be passive people, doormats for the world to walk all over. Certainly not. Consider Jesus. Was He a doormat? No way! Ask the Pharisees![14] But did He argue over everything? No. He had plenty of opportunities to do so; just about every word that passed His lips had the potential to start a heated debate. Often, rather than be led into an argument by an aggressive person, He would ask them a question,[15] or remain silent.[16]

If you argue with God you'll win – because God doesn't argue with you! Those are the kinds of arguments you don't want to win, arguments that end with God's silence saying, "All right, have it your way."

VIOLENT

Violent fathering (different from responsible parental discipline) means that your father was violent just for the sake of being violent. Were you beaten just for being in the wrong place at the wrong time, depending on your father's moods? If your belief is that "fathers hurt you" then it is easy to develop a belief that God "the Father" will hurt you if you get it wrong, or if you believe that He is "in a mood."

You subconsciously live your life waiting for the inevitable punishment that you expect from God your "Father." You perceive Him to be primed and ready instantly to punish everyone who might in some way offend Him. Even the disciples had a view similar to this, and Jesus had to correct them! In Luke chapter 9 we read this account:

> And he sent messengers on ahead, who went into a Samaritan village to get things ready for him; but the people there did not welcome him, because he was heading for Jerusalem. When the disciples James and John saw this, they asked, "Lord, do you want us to call fire down from heaven to destroy them?" But Jesus turned and rebuked them.
>
> (Luke 9:52–55)

This was God in human form.[17] Your Heavenly Father chooses peace over force. If force is needed, then God will use force, as when Jesus made a whip and aggressively cleared the temple of the money-changers. He will use strong words when such are required. His words stung the cold religious Pharisees. The "sinners," however, including the drunkards, the prostitutes, and the corrupt tax-collectors, along with the blind, the deaf, and the lepers, knew they were loved in a way that they had never experienced before, and the Pharisees wanted to stop Him. They behaved coldly towards the people, believing that they were reflecting and representing God. They didn't know that God was in their midst and that they were rebuking Him!

God wants to love you, not humiliate you, or beat you, or violate you.

That's why the Scriptures declare that "God is love" and that's why again and again and again the Scriptures declare that He is the "God of peace."[18]

SELFISH

Another hindrance to fully understanding the heart of God is having had a selfish father – a father who first met his own needs before ever seeing to your needs. You were seen as an unwelcome drain on his resources. Whether it was spoken or unspoken, you were made to feel the one responsible for stopping your parents having a better lifestyle. The result is that you believe that you are a second-class citizen.

You will probably view Father God as someone who will use you for His own ends, because to you that is what fathers do. When the Bible speaks of God giving gifts, it just floats over your head; it means nothing to you. The truth remains, however, that our Heavenly Father is a Giver. He is a Giver of good gifts – expensive gifts.

> For God so loved the world that he *gave* his one and only Son, that whoever believes in him shall not perish but have eternal life.
>
> (John 3:16, emphasis mine)

NEGLECTFUL

Neglectful fathering often results in a belief that your needs do not matter to God. This can sadly then lead to the belief that your Father in heaven will not provide for your needs. To you, fathers just don't care about their children's situation. They seem to turn a blind eye to any distress.

I had a father who looked after my two sisters and me to the very best of his ability. So when God asked me to leave work, I had no problem in trusting God that He would provide, because to me, fathers provide. Yet my wife Linda, who didn't have that type of father, initially struggled to trust that Father God would meet our family's needs. You see, the type of fathering we receive will have a massive impact on how we later relate to Father God.

I clearly remember hearing the testimony of a Christian woman who had nearly attempted suicide. While she was growing up, her father had kept greyhounds for racing, and all the family money went on making sure these dogs had the very best of everything. As a result, this woman, when she was a little girl, got nothing. The only outfit she ever had was her school uniform. So when she went out with her friends to teenage events such as dances, she had to wear her school uniform. To her, it was made clear that a dog was more important than she was. Praise God, her eyes were opened to the real heart of Father God, but it was a close-run thing. That woman's fathering had been so selfish that it had nearly cost her very life.

The Apostle Paul wrote:

> And my God will meet all your needs according to his glorious riches in Christ Jesus.
>
> (Philippians 4:19)

God has never turned a blind eye to your circumstances, regardless of what you think. King David observed:

> How precious to me are your thoughts, O God!
>   How vast is the sum of them!
> Were I to count them,
>   they would outnumber the grains of sand . . .
>
> (Psalm 139:17–18a)

Your Heavenly Father has never stopped thinking about you. Ever. And don't think you just came on God's radar when you became a Christian. He chose you before the foundation of the world.[19] He knew you when you were conceived in your mother's womb, being incredibly knit together in that secret place.[20] God has always been thinking of you – thinking good thoughts about you and for you.

> "For I know the plans I have for you," declares the LORD, "plans to prosper you and not to harm you, plans to give you hope and a future."
>
> (Jeremiah 29:11)

UNLOVING

"The hunger for love is much more difficult to remove than the hunger for food" (Mother Teresa).

Unloving fathering can be an obvious problem. You may have been given all the material things in the world that you needed and even wanted, but deep down, you knew that your father did not love you. As a child you always assumed that you were the problem. As a child you could see how other parents loved their children, but since your parents didn't show you that same kind of love, your assumption was that you were the problem, that you must be unlovable.

This belief that you were, and still are, unlovable, can then result in the belief that Father God can't love you either. You might be able to grasp the idea of God loving the world, but *you*, just you on your own – no. If you have grown up believing that you are unlovable, then you most probably do not love yourself in any way, shape, or form. If *you* don't love *you* then it is hard to imagine someone else, especially God, loving you. To think Father God could love you seems ridiculous. You're right – it is ridiculous. It's ridiculous that He loves me as well, but He does. He loves us in spite of who we are, not because of who we are. If you've been trying to earn God's love it's time you stopped. God's love isn't earned; it can only be received.

For if, when we were God's enemies, we were reconciled to him through the death of his Son, how much more, having been reconciled, shall we be saved through his life!

(Romans 5:10)

This is how God showed his love among us: He sent his one and only Son into the world that we might live through him.

(1 John 4:9)

HARSH

Another potential blockage to understanding the heart of God can be harsh fathering. This can ultimately lead to the belief that God is just an angry judge with a big stick, waiting to punish you for every mistake you make. The thought of receiving love from a father does not match up with your experiences of fathers.

Good fathers discipline their children; only cruel fathers lay down no boundaries or consequences. However, discipline from God is never harsh or heavy-handed or out of proportion. Proper discipline from God is actually very reassuring, as the Bible says:

If you are not disciplined (and everyone undergoes discipline), then you are illegitimate children and not true sons. Moreover, we have all had human fathers who disciplined us and we respected them for it . . . Our fathers disciplined us for a little while as they thought best; but God disciplines us for our good, that we may share in his holiness. No discipline seems pleasant at the time, but painful. Later on, however, it produces a harvest of righteousness and peace for those who have been trained by it.

(Hebrews 12:8–11)

CRITICAL

If you had a father who was always criticizing you, then this can lead you to think that God "the Father" sets standards that you could never reach. That God is never happy with your efforts but always thinking negative thoughts towards you.

When I was in Lithuania, much to my surprise, I was asked by a very well-respected pastor to minister to him. I enquired what the problem was. He told me that he was a terrible pastor.

"That's not what I hear about you," I responded. "Everyone speaks very highly of you. Why do you say that you're a terrible pastor?"

The man said, "I can never keep my office tidy. One day I shouted at a member of staff, and another time, even though I didn't say anything at the time, I had angry thoughts about a visiting American speaker."

I asked the pastor, "Why did you shout at your member of staff?"

He explained that his secretary was always trying to control him, telling him who to see and who not to see, and one day he just got so annoyed he snapped and told her to "Stop it!"

"What about the visiting American speaker?" I asked.

"You can see for yourself that we have little in the way of money or property here, yet the preacher was telling the people that God prospers His people with lots of money. When I looked at my congregation their heads had dropped because they have little or nothing. I didn't say anything to him but I was angry."

I considered carefully what this man had told me. I finally said to him, "Was your father a perfectionist? No matter what you did, was he always telling you that there was always a better way of doing it?"

"Yes, absolutely," said the pastor. "Nothing I did was ever good enough for him."

I continued, "So you think that your Heavenly Father is just like your earthly father, don't you?"

Suddenly the man began to realize what had been happening.

I prayed, "In Jesus' name, I break the measuring stick that has been held against your life. Go now and enjoy your Heavenly Father, who is your biggest Encourager." The pastor's life and his relationship with God the Father were transformed.

With God, perfection is not a requirement for family membership. If it was, then God's family would forever be non-existent apart from Jesus! The amazing grace, the forgiveness, the patience, the kindness, and the faithfulness that God pours out upon us through Jesus does not free us up to sin more, and so throw it all back in His face, but it frees us up to sin less. We are loved by Him and we love Him.[21] Oneness.[22]

> For the grace of God that brings salvation has appeared to all men. It teaches us to say "No" to ungodliness and worldly passions, and to live self-controlled, upright and godly lives in this present age.
>
> (Titus 2:11–12)

Speed limits on our roads are right and good, but have you tried keeping within those good laws every day of your life? If I am driving happily along the road at 45 mph and see a road sign telling me that the speed limit on the road is 30 mph, I suddenly realize that I am breaking the law. I could be charged with speeding (and I confess that I have twice been caught doing so!). Without that "law" I was happy, even though I understand that it is a good law.

Thus the power of sin is in the very law of God itself.[23] God's laws are good laws, but the truth is that, by nature, we are all law-breakers.[24]

> What shall we say, then? Is the law sin? Certainly not! Indeed I would not have known what sin was except through the law.
>
> (Romans 7:7)

Due to the Fall[25] and the subsequent sin-nature, it seems that whenever we are told not to do a certain thing, something inside us says, "But I want to do it!" Forbidden fruit always looks more appealing. The Apostle Paul wrote regarding this very point,

> But sin, seizing the opportunity afforded by the commandment, produced in me every kind of covetous desire. For apart from law, sin is dead.
>
> (Romans 7:8)

It is by the "righteous" law that we become fully aware of this deadly, destructive, unrighteous sin-nature within us, and it is this relentless sin-nature that we need to be saved from.[26]

God always knew that humankind would be unable to keep every law, every day, every week, every month, and every year, but we have to find that out for ourselves. The people we read about in the Old Testament all tried and failed. They constantly had to sacrifice bulls, sheep, goats, and pigeons to "cover" their sins. The law was outside themselves, and they had no power within themselves to obey.

A once-for-all-time sacrifice was desperately needed. A Lamb to take away the sins of the world.[27] A Savior – and that Savior's Spirit within us to enable us to grow in His grace and live God-honoring lives.[28] We only desire, we only long for, and we only accept a Savior when we realize that we need to be saved in the first place.

Living free from the daily demands of the law, but instead living in the grace and the power of God, frees us to live godly lives much more than we ever could by striving to live under the law. The law itself is brilliant, not because it brings us to God, but because it brings us the end of ourselves. Do you sense the Father's heart?

JUDGMENTAL

Perhaps you had a father who always compared you to other people, and you always came out worse in those comparisons. This can lead you to believe that you are inferior to others. Consequently, you may think that you will never be a good Christian. You imagine God is comparing you to other Christians and you see yourself as always failing miserably.

God is not interested in rating you against other people, and not interested in comparing you to other believers.

> An argument started among the disciples as to which of them would be the greatest. Jesus, knowing their thoughts, took a little child and made him stand beside him. Then he said to them, "Whoever welcomes this little child in my name welcomes me; and whoever welcomes me welcomes the one who sent me. For he who is least among you all – he is the greatest."
>
> (Luke 9:46–48)

God wants you to do your best, but what your best is will be different from what other people's best is. Take art, for example. What you draw as an adult will probably be better than the scribbles you drew as an infant, but as an infant those scribbles were the best you could do. So it is in your faith. What you can manage in your early Christian life will be different from what you are capable of many years down the line. Every day, determine within yourself to try and do your best, not because you have to, but because you want to.

Consider fruit trees. You never hear them straining to produce fruit, trying to muster all their ability to make something good. No, they simply cooperate with the life force that is within them already. So with us: to produce good spiritual fruit it is just a matter of cooperating with the life that is in us.

> I [Jesus] am the vine; you are the branches. If a man remains in me and I in him, he will bear much fruit; apart from me you can do nothing.
>
> (John 15:5)

CONTROLLING

A controlling father is a father who dictated and controlled everything in your life, a father who decided – even when you reached a level of maturity – what you would do, where you would go, and who you would go with. This suffocating level of control can result in you being unable to make decisions for yourself. It can result in passivity. Others have to make your decisions for you because you feel that you will probably make the wrong decision if it's left up to you.

It would only be natural then to think that Father God would want to control you, because to you, that's what fathers do. In reality, God does not want to control you – He wants to lead you. He honors your free-will choice, but He deeply desires that you choose the right path.

> "Come, *follow me*," Jesus said, "and I will make you fishers of men."
> (Matthew 4:19, emphasis mine)

Think how many times the Scriptures say, "If you . . . " For example:

> *If you* make the Most High your dwelling . . .
> (Psalm 91:9, emphasis mine)

He gave you free-will choice. A controller doesn't do that.

OVER-PROTECTIVE

An over-protective father can lead you to have an abnormal fear of the outside world and its dangers. This can lead to a view that God the Father wants to restrict you, to closet you in, to hide you away. God is a protective Father, but fathers who overly protect and "cotton wool" their children do so because they are driven by a parent's natural fear of something bad befalling their children. Trying to keep your child from ever experiencing the world outside is understandable, but unrealistic and unhealthy.

If you visited my home when our four children were all at an age when they might be outside in the garden, and you saw them all doubly wrapped up against the weather, sitting talking nervously on the garden seat, you might well feel sorry for them. You might also think less of me as a father. However, if you saw them climbing trees, running, talking, and laughing together, you would know they were growing up in a healthy environment, and you would think more of me as a father.

Don't think that God wants to restrict you. God wants to give you abundant life.[29] When Jesus said "Follow Me" to Peter, James, John and the others, He led them on the adventure of their lives, with good days and bad days, with mountaintop and valley experiences.[30] Yet God the Father was always with them. He is with you when you pass through the waters and the fire.[31] How could we go into the world, to all people groups,[32] and how could we reach the unloved and the unlovely,[33] and be witnesses for Him, if He restricted us? Listen to these words from God:

> I will be with him in trouble,
>   I will deliver him and honor him.
> With long life will I satisfy him
>   and show him my salvation.
>
> (Psalm 91:15b–16)

Notice God says, "I will be with him *in trouble*." He does not say, "I will keep him from ever experiencing trouble." It is a similar truth to that found in the famous passage in Psalm 23:

> Even though I walk
>   through the valley of the shadow of death,
> I will fear no evil,

for you are with me;
your rod and your staff,
they comfort me.

You prepare a table before me
in the presence of my enemies . . .

(Psalm 23:4–5)

God does not us hide us from this sinful world, but rather He goes with us into all the world.[34] Much better!

Go for it!

SPOILS HIS CHILDREN

A father who spoils his child can, even when he has the best intentions at heart, cause the child to believe that they can have whatever they want, when they want it. So when it comes to relating to Father God, He is seen as some sort of "sugar daddy" who will just give you whatever you feel like at that particular moment in time. This has led to seasons of foolishness within the Body of Christ when people have been taught to "name it and claim it" – or "blab it and grab it" as some dissenters put it!

God is a generous Father who gives beyond our basic needs, but He is not like the mythical Santa Claus. He will never spoil us. That's wisdom. We all know what we think of spoilt children.

UNPREDICTABLE

The last example to ponder is a father who was unpredictable. What was right by him one day was wrong the next. Such a father would be led by mood swings and emotions rather than by common sense or reason. This can cause someone to think that they can never get anything right because the rules keep changing. Do you remember this sad line from the poem in Chapter 1?

> *We weren't allowed to get it right because you kept changing all the rules . . .*

A resulting belief may be that Father God is inconsistent. Perhaps you secretly think that God has moods and is led by His emotions. You select portions of Scripture which seem to back up this belief that God is inconsistent: one moment angry, the next compassionate.

God is consistent; He has been since the beginning. Jesus, in whom "all the fullness of the Deity lives,"[35] is "the same yesterday and today and for ever."[36] I have heard people say that God can do what He wants. That is almost true. There is one thing God cannot do: He cannot break a promise. That would be a lie, and God cannot lie.[37]

* * *

From this brief look at imperfect fathering, you can see how it can greatly color your view of both yourself and your Heavenly Father. Perhaps you experienced one or two of these destructive behaviors. You may well be guilty of one or two of them yourself. I certainly did not get fathering right with my children, especially in the early years.

Exposing deceptive beliefs is the first stage to correcting them and going free. As Jesus said, "Then you will know the truth, and the truth will set you free."[38]

It might be a good idea to *put the book down at this stage and reflect* on how your earthly fathering might have affected your thinking on the character of God, your forever Father. Maybe even write the details down.

This prayer might also be helpful:

> *Daddy God, as an act of my free will I thank You for the father and mother You chose to bring me into this world through. I*

do not agree with everything they did to me, but where they knowingly or unknowingly hurt me, I choose to forgive them.

Your Word asks me to "honor" my father and mother so that my days may be long. Daddy God, because You love me, I choose to honor my parents.

Thank You, Lord Jesus, that You show me the true heart and nature of our Heavenly Father.

Amen

Notes

1. Romans 8:16.
2. Psalm 42:7.
3. Matthew 25:21.
4. Matthew 3:17.
5. Isaiah 28:10.
6. Romans 8:29.
7. Matthew 19:13–15.
8. John 14:9.
9. John 10:10.
10. 1 Samuel 13:14.
11. John 10:10.
12. 1 John 3:8b.
13. Romans 15:33.
14. Matthew 12:34.
15. Mark 11:29.
16. Matthew 26:63.
17. Colossians 2:9.
18. Romans 15:33; 16:20; Philippians 4:9; 1 Thessalonians 5:23; Hebrews 13:20.
19. Ephesians 1:4.
20. Psalm 139:13–16.
21. 1 John 4:19.
22. John 17:20–22.
23. 1 Corinthians 15:56b.
24. Romans 3:23.
25. Genesis 3:6.
26. Romans 3:20.
27. John 1:29.
28. Romans 8:10–12.
29. John 10:10.
30. Matthew 17.
31. Isaiah 43:2.
32. Matthew 28:19–20.
33. Matthew 25:40.
34. Matthew 28:19–20.
35. Colossians 2:9.
36. Hebrews 13:8.
37. Numbers 23:19.
38. John 8:32.

CHAPTER 10

THE FAMILY TREE

Come with me on a journey through the Biblical timeline. Along the way we will meet the good, the bad, and the ugly.

The Bible tells it as it is. It doesn't flower something up when it's rotten. As we would say in Northern Ireland, it "calls a spade a spade." So some of the characters we will briefly look at on our journey will be shown to have behaved quite shockingly at times.

We'll start way back in the year 1729 BC (I got these dates from Bible reference notes). This means 1,729 years before Christ, so we're starting our journey more than 3,700 years ago.

Picture a small community in the Middle East. There was a well-known man in this community called Judah, whose son died, leaving him with a widowed daughter-in-law. As the head of the family household, Judah told the woman to go back to her own father's household until his remaining son was of a marriageable age, at which point he would marry her. That's the way things were in those days of small communities. However, time passed and it became clear to the daughter-in-law, whose name was Tamar, that her father-in-law had no intention of marrying her to his son, so she came up with a devious plan.

She dressed herself as a shrine prostitute and, with her face hidden, positioned herself in a roadside place where she knew her father-in-law would eventually pass by. As a widower himself, Judah was indeed taken by the allurement of this "prostitute" and slept with her, not knowing her true identity. As payment for "her services" he promised her a young goat from his flock, and, as a guarantee of supplying the goat, he left her his signet, his cord, and his staff, all of which would be redeemed when she received the goat.

In due time a friend took the young goat to that roadside, but when he got there the prostitute was nowhere to be found. It seemed as though Judah's signet, cord, and staff were forever gone.

As a result of this meeting, Tamar became pregnant. When word of this reached Judah he was furious and demanded that his daughter-in-law be aptly punished. "Bring her out and burn her!" he said. (Steven Spielberg would enjoy filming the scene that followed!)

Standing before Judah and the elders, Tamar revealed that the father of the child she now carried was the man who had given her this signet, cord, and staff. (Can you picture the reaction from Judah, and from the men standing around him?) Judah had no defense to offer, and after recovering from his shock and disgrace announced to all that his daughter-in-law was in fact more righteous than he, and that he had indeed broken his word to her by refusing to give her his remaining son in marriage.

In time twins were born, called Perez and Zerah.

It's a pretty sick story about a couple of self-centered, immoral, scheming, hypocritical people, and you will find their story in Genesis chapter 38. Now we move on.

It's 1451 BC and we have come forward in our timeline by 278 years to the busy, prosperous, bustling, well-protected city of Jericho. It is understood that the walls were so thick that you could have held chariot races upon them. Indeed the walls were so thick that people could live in homes built into the walls themselves.

Down at the end of one particular seedy street, in a house with a window looking out of the city wall, lived a prostitute called Rahab.

Although she was a citizen of that city, she had no hesitation in protecting spies sent in from an approaching army. An army that planned to kill every member of her city. She believed that this invading force could take the town and so she made a deal with the spies that would guarantee the safety of her father, mother, brother, and sisters should the city fall.

Either way she was safe, so it was a good deal. If they didn't win, she was safe because no one knew that she had made the deal. If they did win, she had a guarantee of her safety. All she had to do was hang an innocent-looking scarlet cord out of her window and all within her home would be spared.

The spies and the approaching army thought she was brilliant. I think it is safe to assume that her neighbors and friends would not have shared that opinion. You'll find the story of this treasonous Canaanite prostitute in Joshua chapter 2.

Now we jump forward along the Bible's timeline to 1312 BC, and from a bustling city to a more rural setting. It's harvest time and we're looking down on fields of ripe grain. Teams of men are moving through the fields in line, swinging their sharpened scythes, while other teams gather the fallen stalks and bundle them into sheaves.

Behind the gatherers come the scavengers: the poor of the community. They are allowed to pick up and keep the precious grain that the reapers miss.

On this particular day an outsider joins the scavengers. A young widow called Ruth. A Moabite woman.

Moabites were recorded in Scripture as proud, arrogant, always hostile to Israel, idolatrous, superstitious, rich, confident, and mighty in war. Just less than a hundred years earlier, the Moabites had conquered Israel, forcing them to pay crushing taxes to King Eglon at the Moabite capital.[1] So it is an understatement to say that the Israelites didn't always welcome non-Jewish people into their tightly knit communities, especially immigrants from Moab.

However, this particular Moabite woman had arrived in the area with her mother-in-law, who was local, and so the young widow was politely tolerated. After all, she was doing no one any harm.

The owner of the field they were in that day spotted her and was clearly attracted to her. His name was Boaz. He asked around and got some details about her, then told the young men to behave themselves properly in front of her, and told her that she was welcome to eat with them during their meal breaks.

In due time he asked the men to "miss" a few more handfuls of grain when they were gleaning directly in front of her, in order that she would do better than normal for a scavenger. Mother-in-law was quick to spot this special treatment and gave her widowed daughter-in-law some advice.

> Wash and perfume yourself, and put on your best clothes. Then go down to the threshing-floor, but don't let him know you are there until he has finished eating and drinking. When he lies down, note the place where he is lying. Then go and uncover his feet and lie down. He will tell you what to do.
>
> (Ruth 3:3–4)

If we read this as a modern-day event with society's current low levels of morality, we would no doubt be quick to conclude what took place. The Bible account does not say what took place, but I think it safe for us to assume that nothing sexual happened. (*Why? Because the Bible never shies away from telling what happened sexually.*[2])

Boaz told Ruth, "All my fellow townsmen know that you are a woman of noble character," and he made sure her good name was protected by telling the young men to make no mention of her night-time visit.

In due time it came as no surprise to anyone that Boaz married her, and it seems that they lived happily after ever. It's a beautiful love story, well told.

No one who was in the field that first day, who saw that lonely foreign widow, could ever have imagined the momentous role she would play in their nation's history. To Boaz, she had a son called Obed. Who had a son called Jesse. Who had a whole batch of sons, the youngest of whom was called David.

And isn't it interesting that when David was on the run from Saul, Moab gave David and his family asylum, probably due to David's ancestral links with Moab through his great-grandmother Ruth. Her story is in the short book called Ruth, which comes immediately after the book of Judges.

Now we come forward again, this time to 1035 BC. We leave behind the stories of an immoral, hypocritical man and his immoral daughter-in-law; we leave behind the story of the treasonous prostitute in Jericho; and leave behind this gentle immigrant worker, this lonely scavenger who found love. And we move to the story of the beautiful adulteress who crossed her family line three generations later. An adulteress called Bathsheba.

Now she must have been a real stunner. King David, handsome, strong, and popular, was not short of wives or concubines. That was the way of things in those days.[3] So it is fair to say that he could probably have had any girl he wanted. Above all, however, he was a man of God. A man after God's own heart. He knew what God's laws permitted and what they did not permit, and he knew that adultery was forbidden. There were no "ifs" or "buts." It was off the menu. A 100% no-no.

Bathsheba of course knew that as well. She was married to a good man. A man of great integrity called Uriah, who was very loyal to his king. Indeed he was ready to fight and die in battle if necessary for his king. He was listed (albeit last on the list) as one of King David's mighty men.[4]

While Uriah was away with David's army, Bathsheba chose to bathe in her enclosed garden. At that same moment, King David – who should have been on the battlefield himself – was up on his rooftop looking over the city. He looked down and saw her. He didn't intend to see her, just the way we don't intend to see some scenes on TV. He had a choice to make: to quickly look away (right choice) or continue to look (wrong choice). He kept looking and lust quickly developed. He sent some servants and had her brought to his house, and lay with her. There is no mention of her protesting, and doubtless both were sure that their secret liaison would remain secret.

Bathsheba became pregnant and suddenly both of them had a problem. Her marriage would be over, and her husband shamed. She would be known as a woman of low morals and would be shunned by her family and friends. If it was discovered that the king had been sleeping with a soldier's wife while that soldier was risking his life on the battlefield, then his popularity would almost certainly be over. He would be detested.

David devised a cunning plan. He had Uriah recalled from the battlefield under a false pretext. The idea was that as he was at home overnight, he would sleep with his wife and then her infidelity would never become known. The problem was that Uriah's character was so noble that he refused to stay in his home that night, since he would not allow himself to enjoy a privilege that his fellow soldiers were unable to enjoy.

David had to think quickly. He asked Uriah to remain in Jerusalem one more night and threw a party for him to attend. There he was plied with drink upon drink until he was drunk. Now, David thought, he will go home and lie with his wife.

But even drunk, Uriah would not.

Now David sank to the lowest point of his life. He wrote a letter addressed to Joab, the commander of his army, and asked Uriah to take the sealed letter to him. Uriah did not know that he was carrying his own death warrant back with him:

> Put Uriah in the front line where the fighting is fiercest. Then withdraw from him so that he will be struck down and die.
>
> (2 Samuel 11:15)

Officially Uriah died in battle, but in truth the king he was devoted to had murdered him. It is a horrific story of immorality, deceit, and murder, and you will find the story in 2 Samuel chapter 11.

We come forward some 335 years to meet a king called Manasseh. Even his name strikes dread into any soul that has read his story, and ventures to imagine what it would have been like to live under his fifty-five-year-long reign.

His father Hezekiah was a good man, a good ruler, a God-fearing man but not always a wise man. His son bore no resemblance to his father and it might be said that Manasseh was the black sheep of the family. He rebuilt the pagan altars that his dad had pulled down and he built brand new ones. He worshipped just about everything and anything other than the one true God.

He burned his sons in horrendous witchcraft ceremonies down in the notorious Valley of the son of Hinnom. He leapt into occult activities with a heart and a half, practicing soothsaying, using witchcraft and sorcery, consulting mediums and spiritists. He had so many innocent people put to death that their blood filled Jerusalem from one end to another. Believe me, you would not have liked Manasseh!

But most tyrants eventually meet their match, and in due time the Assyrian king came on the scene and knocked the stuffing out of Manasseh and his army, and took the customary delight in humiliating him. With hooks and bronze fetters he was dragged off to Babylon, his arrogant pride in tatters, and there, in the pit of despair, he finally repented and turned his back on his evil ways. In – what is to us – unimaginable mercy, God forgave him and brought him back to Jerusalem. There he removed all the pagan altars and activities and replaced the altar of God.

Heavy stuff. You can read all about it in 2 Chronicles chapter 33 or 2 Kings chapter 21.

Now we come to only 4 BC, though in truth I'm not sure how accurate this date is.

In the sixth century AD a monk was appointed to calculate the date of the birth of Jesus Christ, in order to create a new calendar that would be divided into two eras: the years before the birth of Jesus (BC, "Before Christ") and the years after His birth (AD, *Anno Domini*, the "Year of our Lord") – and he got the dates wrong! Everyone agrees on that, but there is no consensus as to how mistaken he was. The most popular estimates are between three and six years out, so I have settled for the year 4 BC.

So it's 4 BC, during the rule of Caesar Augustus, and we come to study a young Jewish girl who grew up in a small town called Nazareth, some 65 miles from Jerusalem. It was a town not greatly admired and there was a popular saying: "Can anything good come from Nazareth?"[5]

She had been betrothed (engaged) to a nice man, an older man, for quite some time, and it was a good match as these things go. Then came the bombshell. She was with child, and the man she was betrothed to was not the father. He had every right to call off the engagement, and for a short while he did consider getting a divorce from the legally binding betrothal. But he didn't. He married her, and did not claim a husband's marital rights until the child that was not from his seed was born.

In due time other children followed, but the townspeople were typical of all people. Stories about the young girl grew and didn't lose anything in the telling. One popular story was that she had had an illicit affair with, or perhaps even been raped by, a Roman soldier from the local garrison. (The BBC even produced a documentary around the rape story in 2002.) She didn't have an affair and a soldier hadn't raped her, but she couldn't go around telling everyone what the truth was because no one would have believed her. They would have laughed at her story.

The young girl's name of course was Mary. The baby was of course Jesus. The Father was God. His only begotten Son, the long-awaited Messiah, *Immanuel* – "God with us" – had arrived. You can read Mary's story in Luke chapter 2.

Why do I tell these stories? Stories that span many hundreds of years and cross many borders, involving the highest and lowest in society. What have they got to do with the Father heart of God?

Everything. Get ready for a major revelation of your Heavenly Father's heart. The Old Testament comes to an end with the closing lines in the book of Malachi which speak of God turning the hearts of the parents to their children, and the hearts of the children to their parents.[6] Then there is silence. Not for 400 days, but for 400 years. Not one recorded word from God. The prophets' mouths remained shut.

There can be several reasons for God's prolonged silence with a nation, a church, a people group, or an individual. It could be that we have not moved on the last revelation we have received, and no more will follow until we take that last instruction – His next growth-step for us – seriously. It could be that we refuse to take seriously the sin issues He has gently convicted us of. Or it could be that He wants the silence to emphasize the next thing that He wants to say.

The latter is the case here.

Suddenly, after 400 years, we have fresh revelation. We have the opening pages of the New Testament, and surely the revelation in the opening pages of the New Testament will be explosive! But no. There, staring us in the face, are sixteen verses forming a list of who was the father of who was the father of who was the father of whom, with a seventeenth verse summing up the list for us. Most of us quickly jump to verse 18 to begin the real reading.

But hold on. The opening words in the first sixteen verses of the first chapter are, indeed, truly explosive. Packed with revelation. Here they are:

A record of the genealogy of Jesus Christ the son of David, the son of Abraham:

Abraham was the father of Isaac,
Isaac the father of Jacob,
Jacob the father of Judah and his brothers,

Judah the father of Perez and Zerah, whose mother was Tamar,
Perez the father of Hezron,
Hezron the father of Ram,
Ram the father of Amminadab,
Amminadab the father of Nahshon,
Nahshon the father of Salmon,
Salmon the father of Boaz, whose mother was Rahab,
Boaz the father of Obed, whose mother was Ruth,
Obed the father of Jesse,
and Jesse the father of King David.

David was the father of Solomon, whose mother had been
Uriah's wife,
Solomon the father of Rehoboam,
Rehoboam the father of Abijah,
Abijah the father of Asa,
Asa the father of Jehoshaphat,
Jehoshaphat the father of Jehoram,
Jehoram the father of Uzziah,
Uzziah the father of Jotham,
Jotham the father of Ahaz,
Ahaz the father of Hezekiah,
Hezekiah the father of Manasseh,
Manasseh the father of Amon,
Amon the father of Josiah,
and Josiah the father of Jeconiah and his brothers at the time
of the exile to Babylon.

After the exile to Babylon:
Jeconiah was the father of Shealtiel,
Shealtiel the father of Zerubbabel,
Zerubbabel the father of Abiud,
Abiud the father of Eliakim,

Eliakim the father of Azor,
Azor the father of Zadok,
Zadok the father of Akim,
Akim the father of Eliud,
Eliud the father of Eleazar,
Eleazar the father of Matthan,
Matthan the father of Jacob,
and Jacob the father of Joseph, the husband of Mary, of whom
was born Jesus, who is called Christ.

The Spirit of God inspired Matthew's book,[7] and Matthew's calling was to the Jewish people. Not easy. In seeking to get an accurate understanding of who you are, the Jewish people like to know the generational line you have come forth from. The idea being, "Know the father and you will know the son." So when young shepherd boy David slew the giant from Gath called Goliath and then led the pursuit of the fleeing Philistines, King Saul did not ask who he was, but whom he was the son of.[8]

So Matthew's task was to convince the Jewish people that Jesus was indeed the long-awaited Messiah – with Yahweh (God) as His Father and Mary as His earthly mother. The Son of God and, at the same time, the son of man. Matthew knows he has to first reveal the genealogy of Jesus as the son of man.

If I was God, I would have made sure that all the great and good, the pure and the holy, were in that genealogy so that the Jewish people would be left in no doubt that this was indeed their Messiah. I would have made sure that Moses' and Samuel's names were in the line-up. That Elijah was included. Plus Isaiah and perhaps Jeremiah. I'm impressed with the very thought of such a family tree.

God had other ideas.

The account does get off to an impressive start with "Abraham was the father of Isaac, Isaac the father of Jacob" (though Jacob was a bit of a deceiver). Then it hits something of a moral bump:

> . . . Jacob the father of *Judah* and his brothers,
> Judah the father of *Perez* and *Zerah*, whose mother was *Tamar* . . .
>
> (verses 2b–3a, emphasis mine)

Wasn't Judah the man who slept with his daughter-in-law, thinking she was a prostitute? And then wanted to burn her when he thought she had acted immorally? Wasn't Tamar the deceiving, manipulating daughter-in-law who lured him into that trap? Weren't the twins Perez and Zerah the fruit of that emotionless, lust-driven, illicit encounter by the roadside? Not so impressive.

But on we go down the list.

> Salmon the father of Boaz, whose mother was *Rahab*,
> Boaz the father of Obed, whose mother was *Ruth*,
> Obed the father of Jesse,
> and Jesse the father of King *David*.
>
> David was the father of Solomon, whose mother had been Uriah's wife . . .
>
> (verses 5–6, emphasis mine)

Oh dear, we've got a right bunch here. Wasn't Rahab the Canaanite prostitute from Jericho? The one who was happy to betray her fellow countrymen to guarantee her own safety? Wasn't Ruth a Moabite woman? The generational line is getting mixed blood. Wasn't David the one who committed adultery with the wife of one of his most loyal soldiers while the man was out in the battlefield fighting for his stay-at-home king? And didn't David have the woman's husband deliberately killed in battle in order to protect his own reputation as a man of God?

And then there is Bathsheba: David's co-conspirator. She is not mentioned by name, but simply as "Uriah's wife."[9]

How's it going so far, Matthew?

Further down the list we meet another undesirable:

> Hezekiah the father of *Manasseh* . . .
>
> (verse 10a, emphasis mine)

We remember Manasseh all right. Mass murderer, pagan worshipper, deep occultist. A king who even sacrificed his own children by fire to the pagan god Molech.

Finally Matthew reached the end of the genealogy:

> . . . and Jacob the father of Joseph, the husband of *Mary*, of whom was born Jesus who is called Christ.[10]

Wasn't Mary that young Nazarene girl who got pregnant when she wasn't yet married, and her husband-to-be was not the father? Not surprisingly, the Jewish people were not impressed with Matthew's declaration that their long and eagerly anticipated deliverer had arrived.

What was God up to?

As we will see, He was up to something so special it may take your breath away!

The first revelation was that God the Father arranged for Jesus, the "bread of life,"[11] to enter this world at the very lowest possible point: a dirty, dusty, fly-ridden earthen stable in Bethlehem (which means the "house of bread") in order to identify with the very lowest, the very poorest, and the outcast. Shepherds and astronomers were drawn there by Royal invitation. Angels were sent to bring the shepherds. A star was sent to bring the astronomers. Between them, they represented the open invitation to us all. For in that honored group stood the poor and the rich. The illiterate and the highly educated. Those from nearby and far away. Jews and non-Jews.

The second revelation was the very mixed genealogical line that God chose for Jesus as "the son of man" (one of us). Matthew's record traced the lineage from Abraham to Mary to show that He was the son of Abraham and the son of David, but also to show that Jesus was a Savior to more than the Jewish people. There was both Canaanite (represented by Rahab) and Moabite (Ruth) in the bloodline.

Above all, perhaps, the very mixed genealogical line was to show that whatever your background has been to date, He identifies with you. There in that royal but earthly lineage was a dreadful list of sins and sinners. Sexual immorality from Judah and his scheming daughter-in-law resulting in twins born out of wedlock. Adultery, lies, and deceit from David and Bathsheba. Idolatry, murder, and deep occult practices from Manasseh.

Remember what happened when the Pharisees dragged the woman caught in adultery before Jesus to humiliate her and test Him? He publicly defended her and then privately told her that He did not condemn her, telling her to go and sin no more.[12]

Manasseh was a prodigal son who came back to God. When Jesus tells the story of the prodigal son, we all know that the father in the story represents His Heavenly Father.[13] Our "Abba."

What about the outcasts of society? God the Father had Jesus go to the lepers, the blind, the deaf and dumb, the hated tax-collectors, and the demonized[14] – and finally to the cross as an outcast Himself.[15] Remember Jesus identifying Himself with the hungry, the thirsty, the stranger, the naked, the sick, the imprisoned, and saying that when we do it to the least of them, we do it to Him?[16]

Then there is His identification even with single mothers. Remember Mary's situation and the stigma that would have been attached to her when she first became pregnant outside of marriage.

Can you see it? Everything He has done through Jesus is to say to you, "Come home." You come from a dysfunctional family line? Jesus' family tree has lots of that. You've lived a sinful life, maybe even a dreadfully sinful life? The Pharisees thought they were insulting Jesus when they described Him as "a friend of sinners."[17]

I'm afraid there's no escape. God the Father really, really loves *you*.

He has made the way through Jesus for *you* to come home to Him.[18] To be in His family as one of His "children."[19]

He can do no more. He awaits *your* response.

This chapter is over. *Pause and reflect.* Then answer this question: What is it that your family has done, that you have done, or that has been done to you, that would make God reject you?

If there is anything you can think of, then please do this: Read the chapter again.

Notes

1. Judges 3:14.
2. Genesis 38:26; 2 Samuel 11:4.
3. 2 Samuel 5:13.
4. 2 Samuel 23.
5. John 1:46.
6. Malachi 4:6.
7. 2 Timothy 3:16.
8. 1 Samuel 17:55–58.
9. The original text just has "her of Uriah."
10. Note: Matthew's genealogy shows Christ as a son of Abraham, in whom all families of the earth are blessed, and heir to the throne of David, whereas Luke's genealogy shows Jesus as the seed of the woman that would break the serpent's head, tracing her line back to Adam, beginning with Eli (or Heli), the father not of Joseph, but of Mary.
11. John 6:48.
12. John 8:11.
13. Luke 15:21–23.
14. Matthew 11:5; 12:22.
15. Matthew 27:46.
16. Matthew 25:35–40.
17. Matthew 11:19.
18. John 14:6.
19. John 1:12.

CHAPTER 11

WHAT IS A DAD?

When I take weekend seminars on the Father heart of God I think this part is my favorite. I am not about to teach reincarnation here; it is just an exercise to get you thinking.[1]

Imagine that you have just died and gone to heaven. You are welcomed home and it is much more beautiful than you ever imagined. Once the welcome has settled down, Jesus asks you to do something for Him and you say, "Of course, Lord."

What shocks you, however, is that He asks you to go back for another run through life, starting as a newborn baby.

"Oh Lord, please let me stay here," you plead, dreading the thought of leaving heaven for earth.

"Perhaps this will make it easier," Jesus says. "I will send Gabriel to assist you, and whatever qualities you want an earthly father to have, I will guarantee that your new earthly father will have all those qualities in abundance."

"For you, Lord, I will do it," you reply, and suddenly Gabriel is by your side with heavenly pen and paper (!). You start thinking . . .

From more than ten years of experience doing this in various countries, let me get you started by having an educated guess as to what might be on *your* list. (When there are large numbers of people in the audience, some lists have ended up with over a hundred descriptions.) Get a paper and pen now and use these or other words to make your own list:

Loving	Kind	Strong	Gentle	Thinks you are special
Forgiving	Caring	Loves Mum	Good teacher	Spends time with you
Honest	Patient	Christian	Good at DIY	Goes for walks and talks
Protective	Shows integrity	Sober	Wise	Unafraid to show emotions
Faithful	Rich	Family man	Generous	Good storyteller
Fair	Listens	Healthy	Funny	Not afraid to discipline you
Proud of you	Funny	Defender	Adventurous	Sets a good example
Etc.	Etc.	Etc.	Etc.	Etc.

A few questions for you now: If you had had a perfect dad like that, would your life have been different? Would you have been different? Would you see yourself differently?

From experience, the answers have always been "Yes," "Yes," and "Yes"!

Many years ago I had the chance to spend some time with a very troubled young man who was addicted to gambling, so much so that he owed money to some unsavory characters. I had one chance, and one chance only, to try and lead him towards Jesus. I asked God for wisdom, and this chapter is the result of the wisdom that I believe God gave me.

I invited him to sit him down with pen and paper. I folded the paper in half and asked him to write down on the left-hand side of the fold the qualities of the dad of his dreams.

It was twenty minutes before he finished, and most of the words above, plus some more, were on his list.

Then I asked him to write down on the right-hand side of the fold the father that he did have. And all the words were in opposition to one another. Where he had "gentle" on one side, he had "brutal at times" on the other side. Where he had "faithful" on one side, he had "unfaithful – left home for another woman" on the other side. Where he had "generous" on one side, he had "mean" on the other side. And so on.

When I asked him if he would have been different if he had had the dad on the left, his answer was "Of course I would!"

"I have some bad news for you," I said. "You did not have that dad."

His face showed me that he wasn't appreciating this exercise so far.

"But I have some good news for you," I continued.

He looked puzzled but interested.

"You can have the dad on the right if you want," I said.

"What do you mean?" he asked.

"Jesus' Dad is the only Dad who has all those qualities and has them in abundance, and Jesus wants His Dad to be your Dad," I replied.

We went through every quality on the list and I was able to show Him from Scripture – and especially from the life of Jesus, who was revealing His Father[2] – that this was indeed true.

Several weeks later the young man repented of his rebellious ways and submitted his life to Jesus. The turnaround was amazing. Immediately, the gambling stopped. He kept attending Gamblers Anonymous for a few more months to tell others about the freedom to be found in Jesus. He even brought the leader of Gamblers Anonymous to my house to talk to me. When several years later he married, he asked me to take the place of his absent father at the top table and it was my great joy to do so. He is now a successful businessman, a caring husband, and a great father to two children.

God the Father did not send Jesus to bring us home to Jesus. When you have Jesus, you have the Father "in position." However, God the Father sent Jesus to bring us home to Him – not just "in position" but in a vibrant, living, day-by-day experience.

With this understanding, listen again to some of the words of Jesus (all emphasis mine):

> . . . that you may be *sons of your Father* in heaven.
>
> (Matthew 5:45a)

> I am the way and the truth and the life. No-one *comes to the Father* except through me.
>
> (John 14:6)

> Do not hold on to me, for I have not yet returned to the Father. Go instead to my brothers and tell them, "I am returning to *my Father and your Father*, to *my God and your God.*"
>
> (John 20:17)

Indeed I counted some twenty times when Jesus, referring to His Father, used the words "*your* Father." Jesus called His Father "Abba Father." So may we. When we are Christ's, we both have the exact same Father.

Two heartwarming stories now.

On 10 January 1962 Dick and Julie Hoyt had a newborn son whom they called Richard, or Rick for short. As time went on they became aware that Rick was not a normal child, and their fears were confirmed when he was diagnosed with cerebral palsy. At first Dick was unable to bond with his newborn son because of the lifelong implications of his disability, but his heart bonded deeply with the child during the night-time nappy-changing duties.

The medical staff advised Dick and Julie to place their son in care but they refused, and sought to raise Rick as equally as their other two children. When Rick was twelve, the Hoyts were able to provide him with a computer through which he could communicate with electronically spoken words. If the family played hockey in the park, Rick had a hockey stick strapped to his wheelchair while someone pushed him. If the family swam in the lake, then Rick was carried into the water as well. In due time, complete with wheelchair and portable computer, Rick was able to attend high school where he obtained a diploma. He then attended Boston University where he obtained a degree.

Later he asked his dad if they could compete in a local race for disabled people, and his dad agreed. They finished second to last, but Dick Hoyt was deeply touched by his son's delight at being pushed in the race. So they raced more, and more. Then in 1990 Rick saw the first Hawaii Ironman race being televised. Consisting of not one, not even two, but three full marathons, it must surely be the toughest race in the world. The marathon distances involved are a 2.4-mile (3.86-km) swim, a 112-mile (180.2-km) bike ride, and a 26.2-mile (42.195-km) run, all under the blistering Hawaii sun and the Hawaii lava fields. Rick told his dad that he wanted to do that race!

Now at this point I need to tell you that in my athletic days, after seven years of daily, some say fanatical, training and competing in many lesser events, I competed in the 1987 World Triathlon event in Nice, southern France. It was only a 2-mile sea swim, only a 77-mile bike ride, ending with a mere 20-mile run. It nearly killed me! I finished in nine hours and five minutes, in the dark, long after all competitors but one had finished. (They kindly gave me a medal even though I was way outside the maximum finishing time and the race was officially over.) There was no way, even in my prime, that I could have ever considered the Hawaii Ironman.

But Dick, at the age of forty-six, started serious training, pushing and pulling Rick in his specially adapted bike and wheelchair. Then two years later, in 1992, Dick and Rick lined up with the world's fittest men and women.

First the swim. As the dolphin-like swimmers raced off across the bay, Dick was swimming steadily, pulling his son behind him in an inflatable dinghy. They finished the 2.4 miles and the crowd were deeply touched to see Dick reach into the dinghy and lift his disabled son up in his strong arms and then run towards the waiting bikes.

Dick put the helmet on his son's head, gave him water, and then they set off for the long, hot cycle leg, with Rick sitting over the front wheel on their specially adapted bike. They finished the bike section as it became dark.

Through the night hours, Dick pushed his son mile after mile after mile, and by now Rick was hanging forward in his wheelchair with exhaustion. Finally they reached the finishing line to – as you might imagine – a rapturous welcome from media and supporters, who had just seen the impossible done. Not only that, but father and son finished inside the official time limit.

The last time I checked up on them via the Internet (search "Dick and Rick Hoyt"), Dick was sixty-six and Rick forty-four. They had finished 950 races together, including sixty running marathons and six Ironman triathlons. They had also cycled some 3,000 miles together across the USA. Rick now has his own apartment. Several years ago they were both inducted into the Ironman's Hall of Fame.

The year 1992 saw another dad being discovered by the media. It was the Olympic Games in Barcelona. Injury-prone Derek Redmond – representing Great Britain – was taking part in the 400-meter semi-finals. The gun went off and the athletes sprinted round the first bend of the track. Suddenly there was what Derek would later describe as a "loud pop," followed by a stabbing pain in the back of his leg. He fell to the ground. His hamstring muscle, the strongest muscle in the human body, and enormously powerful in a highly trained world-class athlete, had torn.

Blue-coated officials raced to his aid, but Derek was so focused on winning that he got back up and started hobbling round the track after the others. After 200 meters he realized that the others had finished and that his dream of Olympic gold, silver, or bronze was finally over forever. Suddenly the crowd saw someone else running down the track towards the injured athlete: a short, somewhat overweight man in cap, T-shirt, and shorts. How he got past Olympic security and past the officials no one is quite sure, but there he was. Then he was alongside Derek and trying to put his arm around him. Derek thought he was another official and tried to push him away, but then he heard the man say, "You don't have to do this, son," and he knew then that it was his dad.

"I do," Derek tearfully replied.

"Then we'll do it together, son," said his dad.

They walked together for the last quarter of the race, with Derek crying, his head on and then off his father's shoulder. All the while, his dad was proudly patting his son on the chest, clearly saying to one and all, "This is my son whom I am so proud of."

It was a bad year to win that particular race, since no one but the winner can remember who won it. Many years later, it was voted the twenty-eighth most memorable sporting moment in British history by television viewers.

Friends were sad to see Derek's plight. Team members must have been sad. His coach must have been sad. But only his dad was driven to get up and go through whatever stood between him and his distressed son. If good earthly fathers can give so much to their children, how much more will God the Father, said Jesus.

> Which of you fathers, if your son asks for a fish, will give him a snake instead? Or if he asks for an egg, will give him a scorpion? If you then, though you are evil, know how to give good gifts to your children, how much more will *your Father* in heaven give the Holy Spirit to those who ask him!
>
> (Luke 11:11–13, emphasis mine)

Try this exercise. Look at this strange picture for a moment:

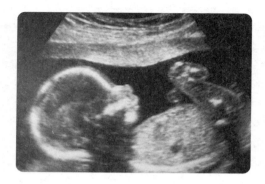

What do you see? The ladies will get it right away. Men might be a bit more puzzled!

For the men here's a bit of help.

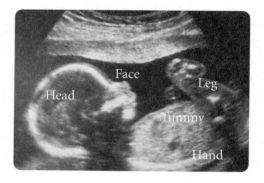

It's a baby in the womb. Now read these few verses from the heart of God:

> For you created my inmost being;
> > you knit me together in my mother's womb.
> I praise you because I am fearfully and wonderfully made;
> > your works are wonderful,
> > I know that full well.
> My frame was not hidden from you

when I was made in the secret place.
When I was woven together in the depths of the earth,
  your eyes saw my unformed body.
All the days ordained for me
  were written in your book
  before one of them came to be.

(Psalm 139:13–16)

You don't know that little baby in the womb, but you have just read something of God's heart for that baby, so here come the questions. From experience, allow me to give the answers I have received back from listeners 100% of the time.

Question: "As you look at that little baby hidden away from human eyesight, do you believe that Father God loves that little baby?"

"Yes," comes the response.

I ask, "Are you sure?"

"Yes, absolutely!"

"OK," I reply. *"But let me see if I can get you to change your mind . . .* Imagine now that that the parents of that little baby dearly wanted a boy (even had 'a word' from someone that it was going to be a boy) but, shock upon shock, a little girl appears. Even though the parents are a bit disappointed with their result, and struggle to accept the child, is that the point where God the Father says, 'I have stopped loving that little baby'?"

"No," everyone replies.

"Are you *sure*?"

"Absolutely!"

"We'll move on, then. That little girl suffers a lot from colic and doesn't sleep too well at night. Both parents are getting little quality sleep. They become tired and irritable with each other and at times with the little baby. Is that the point where God the Father says, 'I have stopped loving that little baby'?"

"No."

"Are you *sure*?"

"Absolutely!"

"Fine, then we'll move on again. The little girl goes to school, and a few weeks later she comes home and is overheard using an unpleasant swear-word that she has learned from other children at school. Her parents are horrified that their little girl could be 'so vulgar.' Is that the point where God the Father says, 'I have stopped loving that little baby'?"

"No."

"Are you *sure*?"

"Absolutely!"

"Now this begins to get a little harder. The little girl becomes a teenager. She enters those stormy, dangerous years. Let's say that she dresses like a Goth. Black hair, white face powder, black lipstick, black clothes with silver fittings, black-ringed eyes. She has friends who are kindred spirits. They listen to music with questionable lyrics. She sulks, is cheeky, and even delights in becoming downright embarrassing to the family at times. *Now I'm getting really interested in your response.* Is that the point where God the Father says, 'I have stopped loving that little baby'?"

"No."

"Are you *sure*?"

"Pretty sure."

"Just *pretty* sure?"

"No, absolutely sure!"

"She starts drinking and taking drugs, gets addicted, steals a few things for money to buy her drugs, and gets into trouble with the police. Tension mounts every time she comes into the house. Is that the point where God the Father says, 'I have stopped loving that little baby'?"

"No."

"Are you *sure*?"

". . . Yes . . . Yes, absolutely sure!"

"She moves into her twenties and leaves all that stuff behind her. She starts doing well. Meets a nice boy and gets married. Has two children. But sadly the marriage hits the rocks after five difficult years and she becomes a divorcee. A single mother. Is that the point where God the Father says, 'I have stopped loving that little baby'?"

"No."

"Are you *sure*?"

"Absolutely!"

"At thirty she marries again, but some of the scars and events and failures of her early life have begun to show up more and more in her personality. She needs a drink or two to escape from herself for short breaks every day or two. Then every day. And, well, you can guess the rest. She has a good husband but is a difficult woman to live with. Friends try to help; some even suggest that she asks God to help, but to no avail. She is on a seemingly self-destructive track. Is that the point where God the Father says, 'I have stopped loving that little baby'?"

"No."

"Are you *sure*?"

"Absolutely!"

"Many a time throughout her troubled life, God has gently knocked on the door of her heart, but she has never opened that door to Him.[3] Now in her old age she has become frail and tired. She needs constant help and attention. There are a few signs of Alzheimer's disease beginning to show. She is no use to man or beast. Is that the point where God the Father says, 'I have finally stopped loving that little baby'?"

"No."

"Are you *sure*?"

"Absolutely!"

"Well done," I say. "*You got it right!* How God the Father longs for her to be His child, to give her life to Jesus, to walk and talk with Him, and of course to spend eternity with Him! But has He ever stopped loving her anywhere along her troubled lifeline? Not a bit."

Now the final question for *you*: At what age, or at what event in your life, did God suddenly stop loving you?

Some years ago I came across a simple painting in poster form that touched me deeply. It was called "Welcome Home" by Danny Hahlbohm.[4] Here it is:

There is me getting a welcome hug from Jesus. There is the Spirit hovering. There are the hands of His Father and my Father, waiting, outstretched.

Get into the queue behind me, quick!

Notes

1. Hebrews 9:27.
2. John 14:9.
3. Revelation 3:20.
4. From Art.com/spirituality.

CHAPTER 12

TIME TO COME HOME

Even with the best of intentions, I can never hope to reveal the
Father heart of God completely, unmistakably, accurately. Only
Jesus can do that, because only Jesus has been with Him throughout
eternity.[1] Only Jesus knows Him as a Son knows a Father. Only Jesus
can reveal Him to us.

> . . . No-one knows the Son except the Father, and no-one knows the
> Father except the Son and those to whom the Son chooses to reveal
> him.
>
> (Matthew 11:27b)

Jesus told stories called "parables" to teach us Kingdom truths and to
reveal His Abba Father's heart. Here is one such package of parables
given to a crowd of listeners some 2,000 years ago.

Imagine that you were there when He was telling the stories. In the
crowd of listeners you would see stiff and stern-looking men with great
beards, wrinkled faces, and frowning foreheads. Many of them are
Pharisees and teachers of the almost endless list of religious laws. Most
of the crowd would have been made up of the likes of you and me: the

ones whom these stern men referred to in their religious self-righteousness as "sinners."[2] They gave Jesus little credibility because He welcomed "sinners" like you and me – and, horror of horrors, even ate with them. The Bible simply says,

> Now the tax collectors and "sinners" were all gathering round to hear him [Jesus]. But the Pharisees and the teachers of the law muttered, "This man welcomes sinners, and eats with them."
>
> (Luke 15:1–3)

First Jesus told them the story of the lost sheep.

> Suppose one of you has a hundred sheep and loses one of them. Does he not leave the ninety-nine in the open country and go after the lost sheep until he finds it? And when he finds it, he joyfully puts it on his shoulders and goes home. Then he calls his friends and neighbors together and says, "Rejoice with me; I have found my lost sheep." I tell you that in the same way there will be more rejoicing in heaven over one sinner who repents than over ninety-nine righteous persons who do not need to repent.
>
> (Luke 15:4–7)

The Pharisees and teachers of the strict laws were definitely among the ninety-nine righteous people in the story who felt they had no need to repent of anything. They were "good upright citizens." The lost sheep, the lost sinner, was the one who repented (said "sorry" to God) and turned to God through Jesus, the Great Shepherd of His sheep. And oh, the sense of God's rejoicing when He had that lost sheep safely on His shoulders and home again. Awesome!

Then came the story of the lost coin.

> Or suppose a woman has ten silver coins and loses one. Doesn't she light a lamp, sweep the house and search carefully until she finds it?

And when she finds it, she calls her friends and neighbors together and says, "Rejoice with me; I have found my lost coin." In the same way, I tell you, there is rejoicing in the presence of the angels of God over one sinner who repents.

(Luke 15:8–10)

The ten coins in the story were ten drachmas, each worth about a day's wages. The woman had lost just one coin. Was one coin – which just one day's work would replace – really worth such a major search-and-rescue operation?

Do you think that your sinful life is of such little value that you are not worth a major search-and-rescue operation? It is well said by others that if you were the only person on planet earth, Jesus would still have come and offered Himself up in your place, to take your rightful punishment, so that you, just you, even *you* could be rescued.

I love Jesus' words about party time in heaven when a sinner turns to God:

. . . I tell you, there is rejoicing in the presence of the angels of God over one sinner who repents.

(Luke 15:10)

Now reverse that. Can you imagine the sadness when a sinner chooses to stay away from God and remain "lost"?

Are you sensing the Father's heart in these stories?

But now, starting at Luke 15:11, comes the big story – the story that the other two stories in this trinity were building up to. Listen in with the crowd as Jesus tells this parable. Imagine the looks on their faces and their reactions as the tale unfolds. Everything in the story was about to clash with their cultural mindsets and behavior.

> There was a man who had two sons. The younger one said to his
> father, "Father, give me my share of the estate."
>
> (verses 11–12a)

Oh, the audacity of the young man, to say, "Give me my share of the
estate"! Since he is single in the story, he would probably still have been
in his teens. I can imagine the men in the crowd frowning and thinking
that no father would do what the boy wanted. It ran completely
contrary to Jewish thinking. In the book of Sirach, written by Ben Sira
of Jerusalem and sometimes called The Wisdom of Ben Sira, we read,
"To son or wife, to brother or friend, give no power over yourself while
you live; and give not your goods to another so as to ask for them
again" (Sirach 19:22–23). But that's not what happened in this story.

> So he divided his property between them.
>
> (verse 12b)

As Jesus tells the story, the shocks keep coming. The young man did
not invest his share of the father's estate wisely in order to produce a
profitable means of earning a living, before perhaps marrying and
having his own estate. Quite the opposite in fact:

> Not long after that, the younger son got together all he had, set
> off for a distant country and there squandered his wealth in
> wild living.
>
> (verse 13)

The frowns on the heads would be getting deeper by the minute. We
might hear "tut-tutting" and murmuring among the listeners: "If that
was my son, I would disown him", or "Shameful boy – a great
disappointment to his good father!"

After he had spent everything, there was a severe famine in that whole country, and he began to be in need. So he went and hired himself out to a citizen of that country, who sent him to his fields to feed pigs. He longed to fill his stomach with the pods that the pigs were eating, but no-one gave him anything.

(verses 14–16)

He ended up working with pigs. That's pretty low in western culture, but let me show how low that was in Jewish culture by telling you one of my stories.

When I was in my mid-twenties, somewhat shy, with a bad stammer, my boss advised me to start taking some of the better clients out for business lunches or dinners. In later years this was easy and even pleasant, but at that stage of my life it was a major challenge to my confidence. I thought of all my clients, and wondered which person I should ask as my first choice. Eventually I decided to ask a young man, only a few years older than me, a young man who had just taken over his father's business. His surname was Berwitz. I know now that that is a Jewish name, but then I did not. Nor did I know anything of Jewish culture. "Naive" is the word I would use. Perhaps "terribly naive" would be a better description.

I phoned Mr Berwitz and asked if he and his wife would like to join me for dinner some evening, and to my relief he said that they would love to do so. I chose a good restaurant. Got a nice table near the window. The four of us were getting on well. Then the menu came. I chose the pork and suggested that they might enjoy the same. They chose something else and the meals arrived. They were grand company and, to my mind, the evening was going very well indeed. This was easier than I had imagined.

Now, to explain my next actions, I have to tell you that if I was out for a meal with my family we would often put a piece of our meal onto another's plate, saying, "This is delicious – try it." (You see where this is going, don't you?) Now, you simply do not do this with clients, but yes, that's what I did: I put a piece of my pork on his plate, saying, "This is delicious – try it."

With hindsight I remember how gracious Mr Berwitz was, coming up with reasons why he was suddenly not "really hungry" and was unable to get even one more mouthful tucked away. What a pity, I thought. Never mind, we were indeed having a good evening.

It was only years later that I discovered that pigs are *so* unclean to Jewish people that if even a piece of pork touches their plate the rest is instantly made unclean. Even though that dinner is safely lost somewhere down my timeline, I would love to be able to go back down that timeline, to that restaurant, to that table, cut a circle out of the floor, remove myself and my seat from the situation, set someone else on the seat, and hoist them back up to the table. But it was me. And I'm still embarrassed.

But back to the story Jesus was telling, picking up what was last said:

> So he went and hired himself out to a citizen of that country, who sent him to his fields to feed pigs. He longed to fill his stomach with the pods that the pigs were eating, but no-one gave him anything.
>
> (verses 15–16)

Maybe the faces in the crowd of listeners were showing some satisfaction at this point. At last the young man has had his come-uppance. Justice is being served up on a big plate. Serves him right. Terrible shame on the family, though. Working with pigs. Touching pigs. Sleeping with pigs. Even wanting to eat the slop that was served up to them. Ugh!

What happens next?

> When he came to his senses, he said, "How many of my father's hired men have food to spare, and here I am starving to death! I will set out and go back to my father and say to him: Father, I have sinned

against heaven and against you. I am no longer worthy to be called your son; make me like one of your hired men." So he got up and went to his father.

(verses 17–20a)

Now the people in the crowd are getting really interested. Coming home to his father? Yes, he is genuinely repentant, but surely his father would never consider letting him come home! After all, he took the full share of his inheritance, went off and wasted it, brought shame to his family, and ended up "ritually unclean" as a pig-minder in a foreign Gentile land.

But while he was still a long way off, his father saw him . . .

(verse 20b)

The father saw him while he was still a *long way* off. That means he must have been actively looking for him on the horizon day after day. If a great uncle who had lived in another country had died and left you a very large amount of money in his will, and his solicitor had let you know that the banker's draft was in the post, then I'm sure the postman would not catch you unawares! You would always be keeping a watch down your road every morning in case this was to be the day your "treasure" arrived.

I am sure many of the men were thinking that if the father did let the son come home after a mighty mess-up like that, it would probably be on a trial basis, as a servant perhaps. The son was asking only for that. He could hope for no more.

But while he was still a long way off, his father saw him and was filled with compassion for him; he ran to his son, threw his arms around him and kissed him.

(verse 20b)

What sort of a father is this? What about a good telling-off? At least a good clean-up from the stink of pigs before he came near the family home. Faces might have winced at the father being tainted with the smell from the son's clothes – and as for kissing him on the neck! Homeless people often wash their face and hands but rarely do they wash from the chin downwards.

Even worse perhaps, the father ran to meet him. Jewish men did not run. This was not for any spiritual reason but for reasons of dignity. A grown man's robe reached down to his ankles. It was regarded as a shameful thing to see a grown man's ankles. For the father in this story to run, he would have had to gather his robes up around his knees in order to get a running stride. He finally draws close to the returning son.

> The son said to him, "Father, I have sinned against heaven and against you. I am no longer worthy to be called your son."
>
> (verse 21)

Even the sternest in the crowd may have been touched by the son's genuine, heartfelt apology to his father. His rebellious spirit, his "I don't need you" spirit, was broken, and in its place was a humble and contrite heart. It's interesting that several times in the Old Testament we read of how God's heart is deeply touched by such a heart.[3]

> But the father said to his servants, "Quick! Bring the best robe and put it on him. Put a ring on his finger and sandals on his feet."
>
> (verse 22)

Picture the homecoming son. His highest hope was to be taken in as a servant. He knows he is smelly. His hair would be long, unkempt, and probably well knotted up. His fingernails long and dirty. Sores and infections everywhere from his gums to his legs. Thin as a skeleton from the famine and the worst of food. The father calls for the best robe. Was it his own perhaps? He would surely have owned the best robe in the house.

What the father was saying was this: From this moment on, I see you as clean as this beautiful cloak that covers you.[4] When we give our lives to Jesus, our Father instantly robes us with the righteousness of His only begotten Son. Then, in the days, months, and years afterwards, there's a divine work to be done under that robe of righteousness, line by line, understanding by understanding, until we start to be as clean under the cloak as the cloak displays us in our Heavenly Father's eyes.[5]

The ring was important. It was probably the family ring with a seal upon it. Members of the family could buy or sell property, and agreements were often sealed with hot wax, pressed with the seal on the family ring. Servants did not have this ancient Visa or MasterCard. Nor did the servants have sandals. Only the family.

What the father was saying was this: You are a full son (or daughter) immediately.

> "Bring the fattened calf and kill it. Let's have a feast and celebrate. For this son of mine was dead and is alive again; he was lost and is found." So they began to celebrate.
>
> (verses 23–24)

Fattened calves were saved for special occasions like the Day of Atonement. So this was no ordinary celebration; this was a feast of immense importance. They even had music and dancing![6] "Let's have a feast and *celebrate!*" the father called out.

Remember how the previous two stories ended?

> "*Rejoice* with me; I have found my lost sheep." I tell you that in the same way there will be more *rejoicing in heaven* over one sinner who repents than over ninety-nine righteous persons who do not need to repent.
>
> (Luke 15:6b–7, emphasis mine)

Rejoice with me; I have found my lost coin." In the same way, I tell you, there is *rejoicing in the presence of the angels* of God over one sinner who repents.

(Luke 15:9b–10, emphasis mine)

Can you picture rejoicing over *you* in heaven? Were you, or are you, a prodigal son or a prodigal daughter to your Heavenly Father?

The only sad side to the story is the older brother's reaction. He had never left the father, never wasted his time or money on the world's idea of life. Yet here is his reprobate brother getting all kinds of fuss made over him.

> Meanwhile, the older son was in the field. When he came near the house, he heard music and dancing. So he called one of the servants and asked him what was going on.
>
> "Your brother has come," he replied, "and your father has killed the fattened calf because he has him back safe and sound."
>
> The older brother became angry and refused to go in. So his father went out and pleaded with him. But he answered his father, "Look! All these years I've been slaving for you and never disobeyed your orders. Yet you never gave me even a young goat so I could celebrate with my friends. But when this son of yours who has squandered your property with prostitutes comes home, you kill the fattened calf for him!"
>
> (verses 25–30)

I know he is "the baddie" in the story, but it is hard not to sympathize just a little with him. I am human and could so easily be that brother. Sometimes when a man or woman has been a Christian since childhood, they can feel a little aggrieved that the ones who are asked to give their testimony in church meetings are inevitably the ones who had the worst lifestyles or the biggest crimes, while they who have always sought to live godly lives for Jesus are not asked to do so. No church celebration or applause for them.

But here's the point. The brother was always home and safe. The other was in the deepest danger. When a drowning man is pulled out from a raging river, there is great celebration. Great rejoicing.

Notes

1. John 1:1–2; 17:5.
2. Luke 18:9.
3. Psalm 51:17; Isaiah 57:15; 66:2.

4. Isaiah 61:10; Zechariah 3:3.
5. Philippians 1:11.
6. Luke 15:25.

CHAPTER 13

WHAT NOW?

W e've reached the end of this book. I pray that by now the old glasses through which you saw Father God are off, and new glasses have been put on. That you are starting to see the Father that Jesus came to reveal and to make a way home to. Let me go back to the introductory page again and see if your response would be different now:

> *Here's a test. Imagine the following for a moment.*
>
> *The angel Gabriel appears to you and says that God would like to see you in His office. Behind Gabriel you see three impressive doors. One marked "God the Father," one marked "Jesus Christ," and one marked "Holy Spirit."*
>
> *"Which door shall I go to?" you ask Gabriel.*
>
> *"Any one," he replies.*

Which door would you run to?

Why don't you go there now? He has been waiting for you to feel safe and secure in His Presence. Find a quiet room. Close the door. Sit on the floor, knowing that He is waiting for this moment. Talk to Him.

Open your heart to Him. You're His son, or His daughter, and He is your Heavenly Father.

Forever.

In the opening pages of the book you read a very painful poem by a lovely lady called Dee Smith. She had suffered under brutal fathering, and, although a Christian since the age of eleven, she could never think of Father God without a deep fear and trembling that literally crippled her life. In twenty years of ministry she was probably the most seriously broken person in this area that I have encountered. It took six years before she was able to complete her Christian journey and come home to her Heavenly Father as His daughter, knowing she was welcomed, wanted, and safe. As I wrote this book I confess that I had her in mind. If she could relate to it, then I was sure that others would too. She did, and I am satisfied. So it seems fitting to finish the book with a more recent poem from Dee.

"The Father wants to see you" . . . the words made me want to run and hide,
Then Jesus said so softly, "I'll be right there by your side."
"But Jesus, I can't see Him, my life has been such a mess,"
My fears, my doubt, my hurt, my pain reflected in my shabby dress.
"Jesus, I can't see Him, You don't seem to understand . . ."
"Sshh now, you've no need to fear, I'll take you by the hand."

The door is quickly opened; the room is filled with light,
And once again I feel ashamed for I look a dreadful sight.
Battered, bruised and dirty, dressed in filthy clothes,
I start to pull away when Jesus whispers, "It's OK – He knows!"
But still the fears of days gone by haunt my mind once more,
Father will be so angry; He'll beat me – of that I'm sure!

I slowly walk towards Him, my heart pounding in my chest,
"Lift your weary head, My child, in Me you'll find your rest."
Could this be the Father? Dare I lift my eyes to see?
"It's time for you to live your life, please give your past to Me!
I'm not like your earthly father; I would never punish you,
It broke my heart – what your dad did . . . no dad should
ever do."

"But what about the dreadful things I've done, or thought,
or said?
And all the doubt and fears that have always filled my head?
I don't know how You could love me, I just don't understand."
Then He got down from His mighty throne and took me by
the hand.

His hand so soft and gentle, He led me to a book,
"Come on, My child, My daughter; it's time to take a look."
Again my head fell down in shame, for I knew all about
my sin,
And the dread rose up inside, what would He do when He
looked in?
He found the page that bore my name, from His grip I tried
to pull,
But on that page in great big words: "THIS DEBT IS PAID
IN FULL!"

I fell down so exhausted from the past that haunted me
And sobs rang out so loudly . . . at last I could be free.
At last I had a Daddy, I no longer felt alone,
And when it was time for me to die, I knew that He would
call me home!

*Through tears of joy I realized the stains that held my dress
together were now white,*
No longer like a battered outcast, but a princess in His sight.
No longer feeling fearful for I knew that I belonged to Him,
*Because His love was such for me, He sent His Son my soul
to win.*
*The Father scooped right down and lifted me, held me in
His arms of love,*
*And I realized that we fit just right . . . like a hand inside
a glove!*

Beloved, I pray, oh, how I pray, that God has used the words in this book to impart into the very depths of your spirit and soul the love that has changed the lives of millions of men and women. The love that is greater and deeper than any human love. A love that was demonstrated once and for all by His Son crucified.

A love that yearns for you, and desires only your love in return.

Beloved. Be loved.

You truly are loved like never before.

About the Author

 Ken Symington, born in 1947, is from Northern Ireland. Although raised in a Christian home, he did not commit his life to Jesus until 1989, at the age of forty-two. In 1994, at the height of a successful business career in advertising, he heard the call of God and left the business world to follow Jesus, wherever that might lead.

He founded Christian Restoration in Ireland, a ministry involved in prayer ministry, teaching, and discipleship training. He has been an associate teacher with Ellel Ministries International for more than a decade.

Ken has been married to Linda for more than thirty years, and they have three sons and one daughter. He is a keen landscape photographer.

We hope you enjoyed reading this
Sovereign World book.
For more details of other Sovereign
books and new releases see our website:

www.sovereignworld.com

You can also join us on Facebook and Twitter.
To promote this title kindly consider writing
a comment on our website or Facebook page, or at
goodreads.com, shelfari.com and Amazon.

Our authors welcome your feedback on their books.
Please send your comments to our offices at:

Sovereign World Ltd, PO Box 784,
Ellel, Lancaster, LA1 9DA, United Kingdom
info@sovereignworld.com

Sovereign World titles are available from
all good Christian bookshops.
For information about our international distributors visit:
www.sovereignworld.com/trade

If you would like to help us send a copy of this book and
many other titles to needy pastors in developing countries,
please write for further information or send your gift to:

Sovereign World Trust, PO Box 777,
Tonbridge, Kent TN11 0ZS
United Kingdom
www.sovereignworldtrust.org.uk

The Sovereign World Trust is a registered charity